Remembrance
and
Prayer
The Way of Prophet Muhammad

Shaykh Muhammad al Ghazāli

translated by
Y. T. DeLorenzo

amana publications
Beltsville, Maryland USA
1417 AH/1996 AC

First North American Edition

© 1417 AH / 1996 AC by
amana publications
10710 Tucker Street
Beltsville, Maryland 20705-2223 USA
Tel: (301) 595-5777   Fax: (301) 595-5888
E-mail: igfx@aol.com

Library of Congress Cataloging-in-Publication Data

Ghazālī, Muḥammad, al (1335-1416 AH/1917-1996 AC)
    [Fann al Dhikr wa al Du'ā' 'inda khātam al Anbiyā'. English]
    Remembrance and prayer : the way of the Prophet Muhammad/
Muhammad al Ghazālī ; translated by Yusuf Talal DeLorenzo

p. 208   cm. 15 x 23

ISBN 0-915957-61-2

1. Prayer--Islam.   I. Title.

BP184.3.G5413   1996
297'.43--dc20   96-38161
                                                              CIP

First Edition • The Islamic Foundation (Leicester, UK) • 1406 AH/1986 AC

Printed in the United States of America by International Graphics
10710 Tucker Street
Beltsville, Maryland 20705-2223 USA
Tel. (301) 595-5999   Fax (301) 595-5888
E-mail: igfx@aol.com

TABLE OF CONTENTS

INTRODUCTION

We Muslims know that, if we seek to attain perfection in worship, we should have a proper understanding of our Lord and fully acknowledge His rights as well as possess purity and refinement. Let me explain briefly. In today's world are whole nations, including some Muslim states, based on atheism, the denial of God. Yet we Muslims, whether asleep or awake, coming or going, feel intuitively that our hearts beat, our eyes see, our hands move, by the will of Allah; we perceive that night recedes, that dawn approaches, that all the wide universe turns, in accordance with natural laws perfected entirely by His power. Thus the distance that divides us from the atheists is scarcely to be measured. Then, there are those whose acquaintance with their Lord is impoverished or even erroneous, who suppose that, perhaps God has a son, or some partner, or that there may be one who oversees His authority, who examines His decrees! Such attitudes show ignorance of the true nature of Allah. True knowledge can neither come about nor be attained, except that an awareness which properly corresponds to reality is allowed to grow through the radiance of His sublime attributes and beautiful names. There are so many who have not even a rudimentary knowledge of Allah. Indeed the world is filled with them —

...most of them believe not in Allah. (al A'raf 7: 106)

— and with those whose acquaintance with Allah is colored somewhat by the truth, but they give themselves the right to act independently without any recourse whatever to divine guidance. But Allah, Exalted is He, requires from His creatures that they be guided by His commands, that their relationship to Him be founded on the maxim of 'hearing and obeying':

I have not created men and jinn except to worship Me. I desire of them no provision, neither do I desire that they should sustain Me. Surely Allah is the Sustainer, the Possessor of Power, the Wielder of Strength (al Dhariyat 51: 56-58).

Thus, explicitly, the duty of mankind is to bind itself to Allah's command and to express its commitment to Him. Allah revealed to His creation an ordered way of life; they chose for themselves chaos. Allah commanded and prohibited not for His benefit, but rather in the interest of mankind. Yet people have ignored their obligation, forgotten their Lord, and legislated for themselves. All to what end, if not to saddle themselves with hunger and fear? Recently, statesmen of the East and West exercised their wisdom so that the earth was about to flow with milk and honey; but their goodwill came to nothing when they directed their energies to developing weapons of mass destruction Finally, the lesser peoples of a war-broken world were left to grovel for the most meager of necessities.

How calamitous disobedience can be! Of how pitifully little benefit! Indeed, it matters not at all how intelligent or civilized the ignorant one may be. Were even half the effort spent on obtaining the necessities and pleasures of this life spent on propriety where Allah is concerned, on the attainment of His pleasure, men might acquire for themselves both the good of this world and of the next.

Whenever I ponder the savage struggle for earthly survival, the tight frowns and the downcast eyes, I am reminded of what the Prophet taught us, upon him be peace. He said:

Allah, Exalted is He, has decreed: 'O sons of Adam! If you will commit yourselves and worship Me, then I will enrich your hearts and deliver you from poverty. But if you refuse, I will fill your hearts with concern, and allow you to stagnate in the poverty of your own souls.'

I understand that certain critics have sought to negate the value of this teaching by interpreting it as referring to those who cut themselves off from society and spend their lives in secluded worship. But these people do not know that the essence of worship is the commitment of one's inner and outer being to Allah, planting one's feet firmly on the legitimate battleground of life without fear or shame.

Worship may be said to be supplication and praise. Within and beyond that, it is the ability to make over one's life, and control its direction, for the sake of Allah, and for the exaltation of His name. Fuller understanding of the rights of Allah on man is more closely connected to the latter than the former part of our definition. For, whereas the former part has to do with knowledge, the latter has to do with imparting that knowledge, with dissemination of its truths, and with its defense.

That was the task of the Prophets and, indeed, that is the task of all those who wish to follow in their footsteps. Proper worship of Allah is a degree of perfection not attainable by anyone merely wishing it. It is realizable only by those who realize in themselves certain qualities of character and spirit. There are those who 'know' Allah. But 'knowledge' is something that differs from person to person in lucidity, depth and substance. And there are those who 'obey' Allah. But then 'obedience' too differs from person to person in ardor, diligence and manner. The station of perfection in worship is attained only by those whose faith has risen like the sun and then flown to the Lord on the wings of love and desire. But for too many, the love of self is allowed to take precedence over all else. From such people Allah, Exalted is He, will remain forever hidden. Assuredly, no person will attain to perfection in worship except that he/she truly loves Allah, for His sake loves others and earnestly tends to their needs, and strives for the general welfare of humanity.

In the domain of scholarship and learning there are those who win the favor of Allah because of their involvement with the truths of Revelation (*wahy*) and their steadfast refusal to compromise them. Of them it is written in the Qur'an:

Become men of God by spreading the knowledge of the divine writ, and by your own deep study (thereof) (Al 'Imran 3: 79)

In the domain of jihad there are also those who win the favor of Allah by shouldering their duty to defend the faith and by refusing to surrender even in the face of bitter defeat. Of them it is written in the Qur'an:

And how many a prophet has had to fight (in God's cause), at the head of many God devoted men; and they did not become faint of heart for all that they had to suffer in God's cause, nor did they weaken, nor abase themselves (Al 'Imran 3: 146)

Certainly the soul to which Allah says, 'Enter among My servants and enter My Garden', is of a very special kind; a soul that finds comfort in Allah and His precepts, chooses Him above all other considerations of wealth or position, and so chooses not on a passing whim, but as a way of life, a definition of sustained purpose, and a direction.

O soul at peace, return to your Lord, well pleased and pleasing (Him)! Enter among My servants and enter My Garden (al Fajr 89: 27-30)

Those who persist in acts of wrongdoing or cling to the fruits of such acts, must necessarily fall short of perfection in worship. Paradise is the resting place of those whose inner beings are pure, whose characters are upright, and whose devotion to Allah has endured. I do not claim infallibility for those who have reached that station. To err is indeed human. However, when the righteous servants of Allah err, they altogether cleanse that error with tears of remorse.

I take great delight in reading accounts of the righteous servants of Allah, and have always tried to gather from them incidents and occasions to give me guidance.

Introduction

In my mind's eye I imagine myself with Moses at Madyan when, feeling the sting of loneliness and want, he cried:

> O Lord! Surely I have need of whatever good You might send down upon me (al Qasas 28: 24).

Or with Jesus when, confronted by the Lord on the Judgment Day, he denies ever claiming divinity: When Allah said:

> Jesus, son of Mary, have you told people: "Take me and my mother as two gods along with Allah?" He said: 'Glory be to You! It is not my place to say what I have no right to (say). If I had said it, You would have known it already: You know what is Yours. You are the Knower of unseen things. I only told them what You commanded me: "Worship Allah as my Lord and your Lord! And I was a witness over them while I remained among them; but when You raised me up, You became Yourself the Watcher over them. And You are the Witness over everything"' (al Ma'idah 5: 116-17).

I imagine myself with Abraham in the arid valley of Makkah when, preparing to surrender his son to what seemed a terrible fate, he appealed to the Lord and Protector of his family:

> Our Lord! I have had some of my offspring settle by Your Hallowed House in a valley without any crops, Our Lord, so that they may keep up prayer. Then make men's hearts fond of them, and provide them with fruits that they may be grateful (Ibrahim 14: 37).

Yet I lose myself completely when I imagine myself at the side of the Last Prophet, Muhammad ibn 'Abd Allah, upon him be peace, as he addresses the Lord in constant supplication. For before him, I feel as if before a limitless genius in *du'a*, a genius unequaled in the *du'as* recorded from the Prophets that historically preceded him. I do not intend by this to put forward some sort of judgment on the relative merits of the Prophets. I am merely stating a fact. I might, for example, say that the tallest mountain in the world is Everest, and not intend by saying so to belittle any other mountain. I mean only to speak the truth.

This book could be described as a short excursion into one of the many pathways in the awesomely vast territory that is the life of the Prophet of Islam, upon him be peace; the way of *dhikr* and *du'a*. Whatever it may contain of value comes entirely from the bounty of Allah, Exalted is He; and whatever it may contain in the way of mistakes comes only from myself.

It is my wish that Allah will accept the words I have put down in these pages and weigh them on the scale of my good deeds; as it is my wish that He accept all the prayers I have made for the Prophet Muhammad, and that He grant each one of us the good fortune to have the Prophet intercede for us on the Day of Judgment.

Muhammad al Ghazali
Qatar, 1980

1

HOW THE PROPHET MUHAMMAD TAUGHT US TO KNOW ALLAH

I am one of the many thousands of people who believe in Allah, recite His praises, avow His glory and majesty, and are strengthened by His bounty and support. I have come to know the Almighty through the Prophet Muhammad, upon him be peace. I read the Qur'an and I studied his biography; then I discovered my inner self harmonizing with his message. My heart and mind were refreshed by his call. Thus I became one of the vast multitude who have accepted Allah as their Lord, Islam as their way of life, and Muhammad as their guide and prophet.

There were people who knew nothing about Allah at all. But Muhammad lighted the way for them, and led them through their own hearts to their true Master. And those who knew Him, but did so mistakenly, thinking that He had a son who could intercede, or a partner who could be of assistance. Muhammad, upon him be peace, came and re-established the belief in absolute unity, refuting once and for all the supposition that Allah could have a son, or daughter, or a partner, or an opposite, or an analogue in majesty.

> Or have they taken protectors apart from Him? Allah, He is the only Protector; He revives the dead, and He is capable of everything. No matter how you have differed on anything, the judgment is still with Allah. (Say, therefore:) 'Such is Allah, my Lord; on Him have I relied, and to Him do I turn.' Originator of Heaven and Earth, He has granted

1

you spouses from among yourselves as well as pairs of livestock by which He multiplies you. There is nothing like Him! He is the Alert, the Observant. He holds the key to Heaven and Earth; He extends sustenance and measures it out to whom He wills. Surely He is Aware of everything. (al Shura 42: 9-12)

No one, past or present, knew their Lord the way that Muhammad knew Allah. Indeed his knowledge sprang from *shuhud*, or witnessing. The Muslim who is keen to emulate the example of the Prophet will be able to discern certain special characteristics of Muhammad's knowledge, *ma'rifah*, in the penetrating and emotionally charged words he used when speaking to, or about, Allah. Clearly there was nothing either doubtful or contrived about his utterance. Lacking within itself a particular metaphorical temperature, the force of human utterance can miscarry and be forgotten without ever having influenced anyone. But whoever reads or hears the words which Muhammad used when addressing his Lord will immediately sense a quickening of his pulse to the flow of those words, and a corresponding rise in the intensity of his emotions. In the end he will have no alternative but to be humble and to submit to the Lord of all the Worlds. I remember on one occasion trying to follow the distances mentioned in a study of astronomy, distances so great that they raced beyond my ability even to imagine them. Indeed, I felt myself growing ever smaller until I looked down to the earth at my feet and thought of what lay hidden beneath its surface. I realized then that I was capable neither of comprehending nor even of perceiving anything. Have we any idea of the number of things there are in this world about which we know nothing at all?

Then, as I was thinking these thoughts, I recalled how Allah, Exalted is He, has described Himself in the Qur'an:

The Merciful is established on the Throne: to Him belongs all that is in Heaven and Earth and all that is between them, and all that is beneath the surface. If you speak aloud (or not, it

2

is all the same to Him), for surely He knows the concealed and what is even more hidden. Allah, there is no god but He. To Him belong the Glorious Names. (Ta Ha 20: 4-8)

The sublime radiance of the lote tree in the seventh heaven and the tiniest seed in the darkest recesses of the earth are as one in His knowledge, may His Name be praised. I found myself so filled with awe for the Great Creator that I was at a loss to put it into words. But by His will I did discover the words to express what I felt. These were words (known from a hadith on the authority of 'Ali ibn Abi Talib) used by the Prophet in his salah (ritual prayer). In the hadith, 'Ali related:

And when he assumed the *ruku'* (the bowing) position, he would say:

اَللّٰهُمَّ لَكَ رَكَعْتُ وَبِكَ آمَنْتُ وَلَكَ أَسْلَمْتُ، خَشِعَ لَكَ سَمْعِيْ وَبَصَرِيْ وَمُخِّيْ وَعَظْمِيْ وَعَصَبِيْ

'O My Lord, for You I have bowed down, and in You I have placed my faith, and to You I have committed myself. My ears, my eyes, my marrow, my bones, and my sinews have humbled themselves before You.' When he raised his head from the *ruku'* position he would say:

سَمِعَ اللّٰهُ لِمَنْ حَمِدَهُ، رَبَّنَا وَلَكَ الْحَمْدُ مِلْءَ السَّمَاوَاتِ وَمِلْءَ الْأَرْضِ وَمِلْءَ مَا بَيْنَهُمَا وَمِلْءَ مَا شِئْتَ مِنْ شَيْءٍ بَعْدُ

'May Allah listen to those who praise Him. Our Lord, may Your praises fill the heavens, and fill the earth, and fill everything between them, and fill whatever else remains to be filled after that.' When he assumed the *sajdah* position (prostrating himself) he would say:

3

اللَّهُمَّ لَكَ سَجَدْتُ وَبِكَ آمَنْتُ وَلَكَ أَسْلَمْتُ،
سَجَدَ وَجْهِيَ لِلَّذِي خَلَقَهُ وَصَوَّرَ وَشَقَّ فِيهِ سَمْعَهُ
وَبَصَرَهُ تَبَارَكَ اللَّهُ أَحْسَنُ الْخَالِقِينَ

'Our Lord, for You I have made *sajdah*, and in You I have placed my faith, and to You I have committed myself. My face lies prostrated before the One who created it, and fashioned it, and opened within it its sense of hearing and its sight. Blessed be Allah, the Best of Creators.' (Ahmad, Muslim, Abu Dawud, Tirmidhi.)

In *ruku'* and *sajdah* before the Creator of Heaven and Earth, an inspired servant kneels and whispers exemplary words, what every being should utter by way of greeting to the Possessor of the Perfect Attributes. In this supplication, one may discern perfect Divinity and perfect servanthood.

Without a doubt, the first Muslim, and that is the station of Muhammad among the Prophets, saints, martyrs, and righteous — was an expert in the art of *dhikr* and *du'a,* without equal in giving thanks or seeking forgiveness. We shall endeavor to clarify this truth by examining something of what has been preserved of the *du'a*s of the Prophet Muhammad, upon him be peace.

Recently I looked again through the Sacred Scriptures of the other religions, and found none of them the equal of the Qur'an in its glorification of Allah, and its exposition of His Splendor and Majesty. In the Qur'an the exquisite names of Allah are mentioned hundreds of times in the course of its narrations of the stories of the Prophets, in its verses of legislation, in its description of the wonders of nature, and in its description of the events of Judgment Day and what is to come thereafter. Furthermore, the Qur'an refuses to allow its glorification of Allah to be merely abstract, without the energy to stir a heart or project a way of life. Indeed, the Prophet Muhammad, upon

4

him be peace, translated the way of the Qur'an in every aspect of his daily life, and became the ideal 'man of God', focusing his attention on Allah alone, and doing everything that he did in this world in His name.

The person to whom Allah has granted spiritual strength and richness will not be shaken by fear or desire, nor by considerations of numerical inferiority or superiority. The spiritually observant person will be equally at home whether alone or at a wedding feast; if his only concern is the life to come he will never be daunted by the setbacks and obstacles of the present life.

The heart of Muhammad, upon him be peace, was constantly occupied with his Lord, immersed in the sense of His Majesty. Indeed, this profound awareness was the basis of his relationship with both God and men. Follow closely his thought in this *du'a*:

«اللَّهُمَّ بِعِلْمِكَ الْغَيْبَ، وَقُدْرَتِكَ عَلَى الْخَلْقِ، أَحْيِنِيْ مَا عَلِمْتَ الْحَيَاةَ خَيْرًا لِّيْ، وَتَوَفَّنِيْ إِذَا عَلِمْتَ الْوَفَاةَ خَيْرًا لِّيْ

'Our Lord, by Your Knowledge of the Unseen, and by Your Power over Your creation, grant me life so long as You know life to hold good for me, and grant me death when You know death to hold good for me!'

اللَّهُمَّ إِنِّيْ أَسْأَلُكَ خَشْيَتَكَ فِي الْغَيْبِ وَالشَّهَادَةِ، وَأَسْأَلُكَ كَلِمَةَ الْحَقِّ فِي الرِّضَا وَالْغَضَبِ، وَأَسْأَلُكَ الْقَصْدَ فِي الْفَقْرِ وَالْغِنَى. وَأَسْأَلُكَ نَعِيْماً لَا يَنْفَدُ، وَأَسْأَلُكَ قُرَّةَ عَيْنٍ لَا تَنْقَطِعُ. . وَأَسْأَلُكَ الرِّضَا بَعْدَ الْقَضَاءِ. وَأَسْأَلُكَ بَرْدَ الْعَيْشِ بَعْدَ الْمَوْتِ. وَأَسْأَلُكَ

5

لَذَّةَ النَّظَرِ إِلَى وَجْهِكَ وَالشُّوْقَ إِلَى لِقَائِكَ، فِي غَيْرِ
ضَرَّاءَ مُضِرَّةٍ، وَلَا فِتْنَةٍ مُضِلَّةٍ،

'Our Lord, I ask You for the fear of You in public and in private, and I ask You for (the ability to speak) the word of truth in tranquillity and in anger, and I ask You for frugality in wealth and in poverty, and I ask You for happiness which is never exhausted, and I ask You for pleasure which is never ending, and I ask You for contentment with Your decisions, and I ask You for the finer life after death, and I ask You for the pleasure of looking upon Your Face, and meeting You without ever having undergone great suffering, and without ever having been subjected to misleading temptation.'

«اللَّهُمَّ زَيِّنَّا بِزِيْنَةِ الْإِيْمَانِ وَاجْعَلْنَا هُدَاةً مُهْتَدِيْنَ. . .»

'Our Lord, adorn us with the adornment of faith, and make of us guides who are rightly guided.'

And still there are those with the insolence to claim that Muhammad was a pretender to prophethood! How they disregard the truth! From the beginning of time to the present, no human being ever addressed Allah with words nobler than his words, nor ever devoted himself to Allah with greater ardor than he. Who then can be accounted truthful if Muhammad was a fraud? The truth is that those who seek to discredit him are themselves so deficient in intellect and religion that they try the patience of even the most forbearing souls. What they say about Muhammad is comparable to what a flying insect could tell you about the suns of the galaxy!

And those who believe not (despite the clarity of the evidence), in their ears is a deafness (so that they hear not), and to them it (the Qur'an) remains obscure; they are (like people who are) called from a place too far away. (Fussilat 41: 44)

6

2

ON A FOUNDATION OF LOVE AND A VEHICLE OF DESIRE

Man's problem is that he is charged with aspiring to the heavens when he himself has been created of clay. Not that he has been created to remake himself into an angel. By no means. Least of all while he is subject to the mechanics of his body and its never ending demands. But he is charged to meet triviality with sublimity, negligence with remembrance, and selfishness with sharing. He is charged, after receiving the gift of life, with dedicating it to Allah. His primary concern is not for himself, but for the Giver of Life, the source of his vitality, and the basis of his ardor and industry! Let me explain this further.

Angels do not need to eat, and therefore have no need to sow or harvest. Yet man, for all his worldly needs, can achieve spiritual equality with the angels if he plants, and harvests, and eats in the name of Allah. Moreover, the time he spends doing these things will be equal in value to the time spent by the angels in reciting the praises of Allah, as long as man does not lose sight of the fact that it is the power of Allah which is acting to germinate and bring to maturity, and that it is through the bounty of Allah that he is fed, clothed and sheltered. From the beginning of creation Allah has sent His Prophets to lead the peoples of various nations along the way outlined above. He did not send angels, because angels have nothing to do with such obligations as human beings have. Indeed, the pagan Arabs were so astonished by this phenomenon that they said:

7

Has Allah sent forth a mortal as Messenger? Say: 'Had there been on the earth angels walking in peace, We would have sent down among them from heaven an angel as Messenger!' Say: 'Allah suffices as a witness between me and you! Surely He is aware of and sees His servants'. (al Isra' 17: 94-96)

The Last Prophet exemplified in the way he lived his life how it is possible for a mere mortal to be the equal of the angels in remembrance of Allah and thanksgiving to Him. On the highest peak to which mankind can be elevated will be seen the ranks of either those engaged in prayer and praise of their Lord, or those *mujahidin* (soldiers of Allah) who give their lives and their wealth in the way of Allah.

Muhammad, upon him be peace, was responsible for creating a whole generation of people to vie with the angels, people who rose above all the attractions of this world to fall in step behind the Prophet; a man who had given himself over entirely to obtaining the pleasure of Allah, whose only call was to Allah, and whose life was summed up in this verse:

Say: 'My prayer and my devotions, my living and my dying are for Allah, Lord of the Universe. He has no partner. Even so have I been commanded and I am the first of the Muslims'. (al An'am 6: 163-64)

No man fettered by base desires, or who sits idly by rather than joining in the struggle to uphold truth and right, can ever know the manner of man Muhammad was.

The emotional and intellectual life of the noble Prophet, Muhammad ibn 'Abd Allah, sprang from the fountainhead of crystal clear knowledge of Allah, from his constant remembrance (*dhikr*) of Him, and from his taking his full share of the perfection inherent in God's beautiful names.

God created Adam in His image, made him His deputy on earth, charged him with developing whatever was good within it, counseled him not to forget his divine origin lest he descend to the level of mere clay, and not to accede to the whisperings of the evil Satan. Since then, the world has not known a man so absorbed in contemplation of the Sublime, who retained his humanity but whose heart was ever in the skies, as Muhammad ibn 'Abd Allah, upon him be peace. He was the finest mortal ever to achieve in his own person, and in those around him, the ideal of the 'perfect man'. His spiritual and intellectual legacies contain the elements by which any man may achieve the ability to perform his rightful duty here and now.

Consider the energy of emotion in this passionate *du'a*. Imams Ahmad ibn Hanbal, Abu Dawud and Nasa'i relate, on the authority of Zayd ibn Arqam, that the Prophet, upon him be peace, after completing his salah, used to say:

«اللَّهُمَّ رَبَّنَا وَرَبَّ كُلِّ شَيْءٍ».

«أَنَا شَهِيْدٌ أَنَّكَ الرَّبُّ وَحْدَكَ، لَا شَرِيْكَ لَكَ».

«اللَّهُمَّ رَبَّنَا وَرَبَّ كُلِّ شَيْءٍ، أَنَا شَهِيْدٌ أَنَّ مُحَمَّداً عَبْدُكَ وَرَسُوْلُكَ».

«اللَّهُمَّ رَبَّنَا وَرَبَّ كُلِّ شَيْءٍ، أَنَا شَهِيْدٌ أَنَّ الْعِبَادَ كُلُّهُمْ إِخْوَةٌ».

«اللَّهُمَّ رَبَّنَا وَرَبَّ كُلِّ شَيْءٍ، اِجْعَلْنِيْ مُخْلِصاً لَكَ وَأَهْلِيْ، فِيْ كُلِّ سَاعَةٍ مِنَ الدُّنْيَا وَالْآخِرَةِ».

«يَا ذَا الْجَلَالِ وَالْإِكْرَامِ، اِسْمَعْ وَاسْتَجِبْ».

«اَللَّهُ الْأَكْبَرُ الْأَكْبَرُ، نُوْرُ السَّمَاوَاتِ وَالْأَرْضِ».

«اَللَّهُ الْأَكْبَرُ الْأَكْبَرُ، حَسْبِيَ اللَّهُ وَنِعْمَ الْوَكِيْلُ».

'Our Lord and Lord of everything! I give witness that You alone are the Lord, and that You have no partner. Our Lord and Lord of everything! I give witness that Muhammad is Your servant and Prophet. Our Lord and Lord of everything! I give witness that all men are brothers. Our Lord and Lord of everything! Make me and my family sincere to You in every hour of this life and the next. O Splendid and Majestic One, hear me and reply! Allah is the Greatest, the Greatest; Light of the Heavens and the Earth! Allah is the Greatest. Allah suffices me and there is no one better than Him to trust in!'

When mere words were powerless to convey the passionate current of his *du'a*, the Prophet had no recourse but to say the same phrases over and over in order to release what he harbored within him of awe, love and veneration for the Almighty. We have on the surface a mere repetition of words, but this is in truth a stilled rapture, emotional and spiritual meaning held in ecstasy. A striking moment in this *du'a* is where the Prophet bears witness to his own prophethood after testifying to Allah's unity and before testifying to the brotherhood of man: 'I give witness that Muhammad is Your servant and Prophet.' This is a way of reaffirming his determination to fulfill the responsibility with which he had been entrusted to deliver his message to all of humankind, however they might refuse to acknowledge him or deny his message.

3

TWENTY-FOUR HOURS IN
A FAR REACHING LIFE

Let us reflect on a day in the life of the Prophet of Islam.

Without a doubt he awoke from his sleep before the coming of the dawn. While the darkness of night still overspread everything, he stirred to greet the first indications of the coming dawn:

$$\text{«الْحَمْدُ لِلَّهِ الَّذِيْ رَدَّ إِلَيَّ رُوْحِيْ وَعَافَانِيْ فِيْ}$$
$$\text{جَسَدِيْ، وَأَذِنَ لِيْ بِذِكْرِهِ اللَّهُ الأَكبرُ الأَكبرُ».}$$

'Praise be to Allah who has returned my soul to me, and revitalized my body, and allowed me to remember Him.'

What optimism, what enthusiasm there is in his welcoming of the day: 'Praise be to Allah who has returned my soul to me.' Certainly the lifetime we possess is a gift for which we must give thanks to the Lord. Furthermore, we should use the time wisely because, as long as we have it, the road to salvation will remain open to those of us who wish to travel it. That is why God favored His servants by creating a sunrise and a sunset each day:

Allah is the One who granted you night that you may rest in it and the daytime for seeing. Surely Allah has bounty for mankind, but most men do not give thanks. (al Mu'min 40: 61)

11

Also, it is an established fact that the key to appreciation of the finer things in life lies in the vitality of the body. What could be finer than to possess a healthy body capable of performing all the tasks required of it without fatigue or strain? Indeed, only then is the Muslim able to satisfactorily accomplish all that he sets out to do. That, then, is the reason for offering praise to God for revitalizing our bodies as we sleep. Let us pause for a moment to consider the last part of what the Prophet said, upon him be peace: 'and allowed me to remember Him'. Such was the decorum of perfect worship in the character of this servant of Allah. For him the gift of another day's life was the equivalent of permission to begin another day's worship.

Thus the grateful servant begins each day in remembrance of his Master with words that literally exude perfect faith and desire.

«اللَّهُمَّ إِنِّيْ أَسْأَلُكَ الْعَافِيَةَ فِي الدُّنْيَا وَالآخِرَةِ. اللَّهُمَّ أَسْأَلُكَ الْعَفْوَ وَالْعَافِيَةَ فِي دِيْنِيْ وَدُنْيَايَ وَأَهْلِيْ وَمَالِيْ اللَّهُمَّ اسْتُرْ عَوْرَاتِيْ وَآمِنْ رَوْعَاتِيْ، اللَّهُمَّ احْفَظْنِيْ مِنْ بَيْنِ يَدَيَّ وَمِنْ خَلْفِيْ وَعَنْ يَمِيْنِيْ، وَعَنْ شِمَالِيْ، وَمِنْ فَوْقِيْ، وَأَعُوْذُ بِعَظْمَتِكَ أَنْ أُغْتَالَ مِنْ تَحْتِيْ».

Allah! I ask You for vitality in this life and the one to come. Allah! I ask You for forgiveness and well being in my (practice of) religion, my life, my family and my wealth. Allah! Cover over my faults and set my fears at ease. Allah! Protect me from before me, and from behind me, and on my right, and on my left, and from above, and I seek refuge in You from all attempts to undermine me.

On the authority of Abu Bakr, may Allah be pleased with him, it is related that the Prophet, upon him be peace, said:

12

Recite the following when you sleep and when you awake:

«اللَّهُمَّ عَالِمَ الْغَيْبِ وَالشَّهَادَةِ، فَاطِرَ السَّمَوَاتِ وَ
الْأَرْضِ، رَبَّ كُلِّ شَيْءٍ وَمَلِيكَهُ، أَشْهَدُ أَلَّا إِلَهَ إِلَّا
أَنْتَ أَعُوذُ بِكَ مِنْ شَرِّ نَفْسِي، وَشَرِّ الشَّيْطَانِ
وَشِرْكِهِ»

'Allah, Knower of the seen and unseen, Creator of Heaven and Earth, Lord and Master of everything; I give witness that there is no god but You, and I seek refuge in You from the evil within me and the evil of Satan.'

With the first signs of the coming day the Prophet and his Companions used to say:

«أَصْبَحْنَا عَلَى فِطْرَةِ الْإِسْلَامِ وَكَلِمَةِ الْإِخْلَاصِ،
وَعَلَى دِينِ نَبِيِّنَا مُحَمَّدٍ، وَعَلَى مِلَّةِ أَبِينَا إِبْرَاهِيمَ حَنِيفاً،
وَمَا كَانَ مِنَ الْمُشْرِكِينَ».

We have begun the day in the way of Islam and with the word of devotion, in the religion of our Prophet Muhammad, in the nation of our father, Ibrahim, the True Unitarian who was never an idolater.

The affirmation of the Companions and other followers that they followed the religion of Muhammad, upon him be peace, is quite clear. But what is the meaning of his making the same affirmation? Indeed, it occurs in countless other *du'as* that the Prophet, upon him be peace, gives witness to his own prophethood or the truth of his mission.

There are a number of good reasons for this. Among them is that the Prophet, upon him be peace, was the first to put into practice the message with which he had been entrusted. So often we see religious leaders who consider their religion something to foist upon others, while they themselves act as if they are above all such considerations. Or he may have done it as a way of forcing proof on the disbelievers and other critics, so as to make of it an established truth impervious to attacks of doubt or conjecture. Or he may have done it out of a feeling of gratitude for the gift which Allah had bestowed upon him, as a sign of his satisfaction and happiness with the position Allah had chosen for him to fill. In any case, from the moment he awoke, his heart stirred with feelings of veneration and appreciation for Allah's bounty; feelings which he would then translate into lucid sentences:

$$\text{«اللَّهُمَّ مَا أَصْبَحَ بِي مِنْ نِعْمَةٍ أَوْ بِأَحَدٍ مِنْ خَلْقِكَ}$$
$$\text{فَمِنْكَ وَحْدَكَ لاَ شَرِيكَ لَكَ، فَلَكَ الْحَمْدُ، وَلَكَ}$$
$$\text{الشُّكْرُ».}$$

Allah! In whatever favor I or any other of Your creatures find ourselves this morning, it is from You and You alone! You have no partner, and all praise is due to You and all thanks!

$$\text{«اللَّهُمَّ إِنِّي أَصْبَحْتُ مِنْكَ فِي نِعْمَةٍ وَعَافِيَةٍ وَسَتْرٍ،}$$
$$\text{فَأَتِمَّ نِعْمَتَكَ عَلَيَّ وَعَافِيَتَكَ، وَسَتْرَكَ فِي الدُّنْيَا}$$
$$\text{وَالآخِرَةِ».}$$

Allah! I awake to favor from You, and vitality, and protection! Then complete Your favor upon me, and revitalize me, and protect me in this World and the Next.

On the authority of Abu Hurayrah it is related that the Prophet of Allah, upon him be peace, said:

14

There is not a person who stirs from his sleep and says:

$$\text{«الْحَمْدُ لِلَّهِ الَّذِيْ خَلَقَ النَّوْمَ وَالْيَقْظَةَ، الْحَمْدُ لِلَّهِ الَّذِيْ بَعَثَنِيْ سَالِماً سَوِياً، أَشْهَدُ أَنَّ اللَّهَ يُحْيِيْ ٱلْمَوْتَى، وَهُوَ عَلَى كُلِّ شَيْءٍ قَدِيْرٌ.. »}$$

'Praise to Allah Who has created sleeping and waking. Praise to Allah Who has aroused me safe and sound! I give witness that Allah will revive the dead, and that He is Powerful over everything', except that Allah replies: My servant has spoken truthfully.

Is it not an excellent thing that a person should praise his Lord and then find not only that God has heard his praises, but that He accepts and confirms the truth of his words, and in doing so, furthermore, recruits that person to His service by calling him, 'My servant'?

On the authority of Abu Malik al Ash'ari it is related that the Prophet, upon him be peace, said:

When you wake up in the morning, say:

$$\text{«أَصْبَحْنَا وَأَصْبَحَ الْمُلْكُ لِلَّهِ رَبِّ الْعَالَمِيْنَ، اللَّهُمَّ إِنِّي أَسْأَلُكَ خَيْرَ هَذَا الْيَوْمِ، فَتْحَهُ وَنَصْرَهُ وَنُوْرَهُ وَبَرَكَتَهُ وَهُدَاهُ، وَأَعُوْذُ بِكَ مِنْ شَرِّ مَا فِيْهِ، وَشَرِّ مَا بَعْدَهُ».}$$

'We have awoken, and all of creation has awoken, for Allah, Lord of all the Worlds. Allah, I ask You for the best the day has to offer, victory, support, light, blessings and guidance; and I seek refuge in You from the evil in it, and the evil to come after it.' When you go to sleep at night, say the same thing.

15

Most people live their lives as if within a cave filled with the gloom of real or imagined problems. And it is really a tragedy that otherwise intelligent minds are able to see no further than the walls of that cave, and that their worry-ridden hearts are able to sense only darkness and constraint. The Prophet of Allah, upon him be peace, rejected this kind of defeatist isolationism when he said:

> Not a morning passes in which the servants of Allah awake except that a caller calls out, 'Praise to Allah, the Sacred, the Supreme.'

In another version of the same narration:

> ... a crier cries out, 'O Creation! Praise the Sacred One, the Supreme!'

It is tempting to say that the heart of Muhammad, upon him be peace, and only his heart, was the one to listen to the crier's warning to mankind to tear away the barriers of neglect and race to the Sacred, Supreme One. Indeed, his skill in arousing others was a direct result of his total immersion in *dhikr* (remembrance) of Allah, and his constant awareness of the Possessor of Majesty.

The scholars of law are unanimous that there is no obligation upon members of the Muslim community to repeat the *du'a*s we record in these or subsequent pages. Their repetition is desirable and commendable, but not obligatory. And, of course, that is as it should be. Yet, so it seems to me, for the spiritually weak, an extended contemplation of these *du'a*s is more than necessary. They are remarkably effective in acquainting people with their Lord and providing them with insight into the meanings of His beautiful names.

Vague or ambiguous faith is of little benefit to anyone; and flagging faith is incapable of directing behavior or bridling passion. The Companions of the Prophet of Allah did not reach the summit of faith, or change the history of the world, or establish a new order, or set new standards of moral behavior, except as a result of their direct relationship with the Prophet of Allah, and the diffusion of sincerity and love of Allah from his heart to theirs.

It is in the nature of mankind that when desire is strong enough it will have the energy to stir the dying fire of failing commitment into a new burst of flame. Listening to the Prophet and penetrating his emotions, as he offers *du'a*, is a sure way to rekindle the flames, to refurbish a smoked out interior, or at least to stir someone into making the attempt to approach his Lord.

The *du'a*s I have mentioned so far have all been of the optional type. There is, in addition, a certain prescribed amount of another kind of relationship with Allah, associated with the mosque; the ritual prayers (salah) which must be performed daily by every Muslim. In the course of every twenty four hours each Muslim is required to stand before the Almighty in prayer five times. Furthermore, the Muslim's presence in the mosque for the performance of each salah is either essential or strongly recommended. Obviously the position occupied by the mosque in Muslim society is a very eminent one. This might be surprising to certain of our people who have lost sight of the importance of salah.

The Muslim's walk to the mosque begins before dawn. As an encouragement, there is the teaching of the Prophet, upon whom be peace:

> Give glad tidings to those who walk to the mosques in the dark of night, that on the Day of Rising they will have perfect light.

> The day when you see the believers, men and women, their light running before them, and on their right. (al Hadid 57: 12)

> They say, 'Our Lord, make this our light perfect and forgive us.' (al Tahrim 66: 8)

Concerning the Muslim's journey on foot to the mosque for the purpose of performing the salah, the authentic teaching of the Prophet is that whenever anyone raises one foot and lowers the other, a good deed will be recorded for him and an evil one erased in the book of his deeds, and he will be raised up one level in the world to come.

Ibn 'Abbas related that the Prophet, upon him be peace, went out to salah after hearing the call to prayer, saying:

«اللَّهُمَّ اجْعَلْ فِيْ قَلْبِيْ نُوْراً وَفِيْ لِسَانِيْ نُوْراً وَاجْعَلْ فِيْ سَمْعِيْ نُوْراً وَاجْعَلْ فِيْ بَصَرِيْ نُوْراً، وَاجْعَلْ مِنْ خَلْفِيْ نُوْراً وَمِنْ أَمَامِيْ نُوْراً، اللَّهُمَّ أَعْطِنِيْ نُوْراً».

Allah! Put light in my heart, and light on my tongue, and light in my ears, and light in my eyes, and light behind me, and light before me. Allah! Give me light!

Indeed Allah granted him what he asked, as he was a 'Caller to Allah by His leave, and a Light-giving Lamp'. (al Ahzab 33: 46)

In still another narration it is related that when the Prophet entered the mosque he would praise Allah, and take His name and then say:

«اللَّهُمَّ اغْفِرْ لِيْ وَافْتَحْ لِيْ أَبْوَابَ رَحْمَتِكَ».

Allah, forgive me, and open the doors of Your Mercy for me.

When the Prophet, upon him be peace, left the mosque he would do the same (praise Allah, take His name) and then say:

«اللَّهُمَّ افْتَحْ لِيْ أَبْوَابَ فَضْلِكَ».

Allah, open the doors of Your Bounty for me!

The Prophet's love for salah was so great that whenever he heard the *mu'adhdhin* say: 'The time for salah has come', he would reply:

$$\text{.}\langle\langle\text{أَقَامَهَا اللهُ وَأَدَامَهَا}\rangle\rangle$$

'May Allah perpetuate it forever.'

As the *mu'adhdhin* makes his call to prayer, we should repeat the call (to ourselves), and then add a prayer for the Prophet, upon him be peace, after which we should say:

$$\langle\langle\text{اللّٰهُمَّ رَبَّ هٰذِهِ الدَّعْوَةِ التَّامَّةِ، وَالصَّلَاةِ الْقَائِمَةِ}$$
$$\text{آتِ مُحَمَّداً الْوَسِيْلَةَ وَالْفَضِيْلَةَ، وَابْعَثْهُ مَقَاماً مَحْمُوْداً}$$
$$\text{الَّذِي وَعَدْتَهُ}\rangle\rangle\text{.}$$

Allah! Lord of this perfect call, and the salah about to be performed; grant Muhammad *al wasilah* (a special place in heaven) and excellence, and raise him up to a praised position (of interceding on behalf of his followers on the Judgment Day), one which You promised to him.

The reason the Prophet taught his followers to say 'a' (rather than 'the') praised position is because he was pleased with the wording of the Qur'an in its promise of a reward for one (the Prophet himself) who regularly performs the salah of *tahajjud* in the hours before dawn:

And at night, perform *tahajjud*, a part of it (the night) as something extra for yourself; it may be that your Lord will raise you up to a praised position. (al Isra' 17: 79)

The Prophet held by the words that indicated the position he would occupy in the next world, and requested of his followers that they petition the Almighty for that promised reward, in compensation for his long nightly vigil of standing, bowing and prostrating himself in prayer so much that his feet swelled up under the strain of it. Undoubtedly the place that love for Allah occupied in the heart of this devoted servant was such that it could never be filled by anything else.

Thus he fostered — by means of the mosque — the men who would lead humanity, culturally and politically, after him. Indeed, the world had never seen a civilization so noble or so pure, as the one molded by the men fostered by Muhammad; a civilization nurtured by the Qur'anic revelation which transformed an unknown desert into an institution capable of producing the most knowledgeable of men with regard to law and values, and the most deserving of spiritual and temporal rule. Those were the men whose hearts soared in awe whenever the Prophet recited the Qur'an to them, and whose eyes were filled with love and respect at the sight of Muhammad, upon him be peace.

It was when the Prophet, in his final illness, looked upon his followers at prayer in the mosque that he felt that he had finally completed his mission. When he saw them there in sincere devotion to Allah, his face lit up like a sheet of glistening gold. This was all he had ever wanted; to leave behind him, when called to meet his Almighty Maker, the living fruit of all his tireless efforts.

Will the mosques again one day produce men as they did in those days? Certainly the structures are similar, but the people inside them are not all that we might have hoped for. Our situation recalls the feelings of Majnun, Layla's lover, when the poet has him say:

> As for the tents, well, certainly they resemble the tents of her tribe. But the women of this place, I see, are not the same!

4
More Than Food and Drink

The Prophets were men who, like everyone else, needed regular nourishment. It is pointless to dwell on the objection of the pre-Islamic Arab idolaters that a Prophet should be above such needs, an objection as absurd then as now. Every human body requires food in order to sustain life. Yet it is true that those who live for the realization of some noble objective invariably sacrifice their personal needs to it and, in their singularity of purpose, can ignore the most tempting of worldly delights.

As for ourselves, we live in times when securing immediate pleasures seems to be the only concern. Certainly, we may find among our contemporaries a few willing to make sacrifices in order to accomplish one or another great project; but rarely will we find one who has made that project the be all and end all of his existence.

The Prophet Muhammad, upon him be peace, and the generation of men and women who learned from him, were of an altogether different spiritual and moral fiber. Consider the following narration:

> One day the Prophet of Allah, upon him be peace, saw 'Umar ibn al Khattab wearing an attractive garment. The Prophet asked, 'Is that new or just newly washed?' 'Newly washed', replied 'Umar. Then the Prophet answered him with a *du'a*: 'May you always wear new clothes, and live a praised man, and die a martyr.'

21

Thus, death in the way of Allah was one of the tokens of felicity sought for 'Umar, along with a praiseworthy life and wealth enough to ensure a supply of new clothes. Concern for the bliss of the next world so permeated the consciousness of those first Muslims that they made no distinction between worldly and other worldly pleasures. Is it at all likely that such men would live for the sole purpose of indulging their appetites at grand feasts?

I would not in any way wish to disparage a man's just pursuit of sustenance, for that is a part of human nature. Indeed, everyone has the right to take pleasure from life's necessities, even to savor its luxuries, so long as this does not implant greed or so ingrain easy habits that the hardships of battle, for the faith or the homeland, become too unbearable to even contemplate, let alone endure.

Undoubtedly, the Prophet Muhammad, upon him be peace, was in a position to command the coarser pleasures of life, in any measure, including those of gourmandising. But there is nothing in the Traditions to indicate that he showed the least interest in fine or elaborate cuisine. Nor, conversely, did he ever order anyone to seek out hardship. He never taught asceticism, and he never prohibited what was lawful. He was, on the contrary, always appreciative of the favor of Allah, and always thankful. Consider this teaching:

> Whenever any of you eats, let him take the name of Allah when he begins; and if he should forget to do so when beginning, let him take the name of Allah when finishing, saying: 'In the name of Allah, at the beginning and at the end.'

And when the Prophet had finished his meal, he would say:

$$\text{«الْحَمْدُ لِلَّهِ الَّذِيْ أَطْعَمَنَا وَسَقَانَا وَجَعَلَنَا مُسْلِمِيْنَ».}$$

> Praise to Allah who has given us food and drink, and who has made us Muslims.

22

In sum and balance, the Prophet taught that:

Almighty Allah is pleased when His servant partakes of food and then praises Him for it, and when His servant drinks and then praises Him for the drink.

But the majority of people fill themselves to bursting and then go about their business without any consciousness of owing something to Allah. Such crass, brute indifference is in no way worthy of a believer.

The Imam of all the Prophets expressed a great talent and variety in the ways that he would praise Allah after taking his daily meals. Among the du'as narrated in the books of Hadith are the following:

«اَللّٰهُمَّ أَطْعَمْتَ وَسَقَيْتَ، وَأَغْنَيْتَ، وَأَقْنَيْتَ، وَهَدَيْتَ، وَأَحْيَيْتَ، فَلَكَ الْحَمْدُ عَلَى مَاأَعْطَيْتَ».

O Allah! You have given food and drink, and You have enriched and satisfied, and guided and given life. Thanks to You for all You have given.

«الْحَمْدُ لِلّٰهِ الَّذِيْ أَطْعَمَنِيْ هٰذَا وَرَزَقَنِيْهِ مِنْ غَيْرِ حَوْلٍ مِّنِّيْ وَلَا قُوَّةٍ»

Praise to Allah who has fed me this and nourished me thereby without my having contributed anything, neither power nor resources.

«الْحَمْدُ لِلّٰهِ الَّذِيْ أَطْعَمَ وَسَقَى، وَسَوَّغَهُ، وَجَعَلَ لَهُ مَخْرَجاً».

Praise to Allah who has provided food and drink, then caused it to be digested and disposed of.

This open hearted acceptance of bounty and benefit, and whole hearted thanksgiving to Him who confers it, has especial significance (in Islam) and deserves some elucidation.

The Last of the Prophets was not afflicted with physical weakness or infirmities, being instead endowed with strength and stamina, capable of facing all opponents, a battlefield warrior who would run to meet the enemy's charge. When being well-built means being able to answer any call to duty, then it is a great blessing and advantage. A fit and healthy person is more likely to look at the world, and deal in it, with generosity and magnanimity, than one who is not. On this ground, he has the right to help himself to what he needs to stay fit and healthy. Allah never prohibits the kind of food that promotes healthy regeneration of cells that break down under the strain of exertion or long life. Whoever argues the contrary is essentially misrepresenting Islam. What Islam opposes is damaging excess, gluttony, obesity, and other derived and related maladies of that nature. Nor, on this issue, is there any disagreement between the prescriptions of religion and those of medical science.

Yet there were many occasions when the Prophet, upon him be peace, had to be satisfied with no more than a few morsels of food, or less, a handful of dates. On one occasion, when he found that there was nothing to be had in the house except vinegar, he remarked: 'An excellent condiment, vinegar!' It is this kind of vigorous, cheerful vitality that keeps the mind unscarred by temporary setbacks, and sustains the body's vitality even when denied that to which it has grown accustomed.

5

THE PROPHET AND THE SOCIAL GATHERING

There are times when a man feels he has to get away from it all in order to preserve his emotional balance or intellectual acuteness. According to most psychologists, people are unable to sustain an optimum level of intellectual activity while in the company of others. This is probably true with respect to most great men. However, the Prophets of Allah were men who were at their best when in the company of others; company never made them 'low'. Indeed, there were those among the Companions of the Prophet who complained that they could not sustain, outside his company, the level of consciousness that they attained while with him. In his company the Companions would become so conscious of Allah that they enjoined His worship on each other and gave counsel concerning the duties they owed to Him. The Prophet detested the meetings of the heedless and unmindful, because of his aversion to any gathering in which there was no mention of Allah. His teaching on the subject is:

> Whenever a group gets up from a meeting in which Allah
> is never once mentioned, it is as if they get up from the
> decaying corpse of a donkey; and it is for them a great
> misfortune.

Thus all those gatherings in which Allah is forgotten and only matters of worldly interest, or pleasure, are mentioned are in effect gatherings of decay. Indeed? What is there about them which deserves to be preserved? The only things deserving of preservation are those which relate in some way to the Eternal One, may His name be blessed!

Whenever a Muslim finds himself in a gathering where the major subject of concern is the life of this world (even if there is some mention of the next world as well), he should remember the following teaching of the Prophet, upon him be peace:

> Whoever sits in a gathering in which there is a great deal of clamor and says, before rising,

$$ سُبْحَانَكَ اَللَّهُمَّ وَبِحَمْدِكَ أَشْهَدُ أَن لاَّ إِلَهَ إِلاَّ أَنْتَ أَسْتَغْفِرُكَ وَأَتُوبُ إِلَيْكَ. $$

> 'Glory to You, O Lord, and praise. I give witness that there is no God but You. To You I repent, and unto You I return', will be forgiven by Allah for whatever transpired in the gathering he took part in.

In another hadith the Prophet, upon him be peace, said:

> If a Muslim is in a gathering where only good is discussed, then that [his reciting the *du'a* mentioned in the hadith above] will become as an imprint (of good) for him; whereas if the gathering had elements of both good and evil, then that will be expiation for whatever transpired in the gathering.

Because socializing might have the effect of stirring up rivalry in worldly affairs, or ostentatiousness, or even arrogance; and because it might tend to occupy the minds of people with trivialities; and because it might make relationships which were better not made, for these reasons, as reported on the authority of Ibn 'Umar: Rarely, if ever, did the Prophet, upon him be peace, rise from a gathering without reciting the following *du'a* for his Companions:

26

«اَللَّهُمَّ اقْسِمْ لَنَا مِنْ خَشْيَتِكَ مَا تَحُوْلُ بِهِ بَيْنَنَا وَبَيْنَ مَعَاصِيْكَ، وَمِنْ طَاعَتِكَ مَا تُبَلِّغُنَا بِهِ جَنَّتَكَ وَمِنَ الْيَقِيْنِ مَا تُهَوِّنُ بِهِ عَلَيْنَا مَصَائِبَ الدُّنْيَا».

«اَللَّهُمَّ مَتِّعْنَا بِأَسْمَاعِنَا وَأَبْصَارِنَا وَقُوَّتِنَا مَا أَحْيَيْتَنَا، وَاجْعَلْهُ الْوَارِثَ مِنَّا وَاجْعَلْ ثَأْرَنَا عَلَى مَنْ ظَلَمَنَا، وَانْصُرْنَا عَلَى مَنْ عَادَانَا، وَلَا تَجْعَلْ مُصِيْبَتَنَا فِيْ دِيْنِنَا، وَلَا تَجْعَلِ الدُّنْيَا أَكْبَرَ هَمِّنَا، وَلَا مَبْلَغَ عِلْمِنَا، وَلَا تُسَلِّطْ عَلَيْنَا مَنْ لَا يَرْحَمُنَا».

O Allah, distribute between us the heedfulness necessary to come between us and the commission of wrong against You, and the obedience necessary to gain for us admission to Your paradise, and the unswerving faith necessary to minimize for us the tribulations of this world. O Allah, allow us to enjoy our hearing, our sight, and our strength for as long as we live, and make that enjoyment our heir (so that when we are gone those who have benefited through us will remember to pray for us), and place our vengeance on those who have wronged us, and give us victory over our enemies, and try us not in our faith, neither make this world our greatest concern or the extent of our knowledge, nor give power over us to those who would oppress us.

In this way the Prophet used to call an end to his meetings. Thus, no one who attended would return to his home without having been immersed in the mercy of Allah!

6

WHITE NIGHT

With the five daily prayers finished, his day over, every man feels free to return home for rest and relaxation. But was that the way Muhammad, upon him be peace, greeted the coming night? Had the great philosophers of metaphysics attained in their days of work even a fraction of what Muhammad accomplished in a single night, it would have sufficed to make their reputations, and been accounted a splendid effort on their part. For the Prophet, the supreme worshipper, upon him be peace, nightfall but began a new stage in the stages of his devotion to Allah. Indeed, on the subject of his nightly *du'as*, scholars have related a great many hadith. Thus, it is related on the authority of Hudhayfah and Abu Dharr that the Prophet, upon him be peace, whenever he retired to his bed, would say:

In Your name, O Allah, I live and die.

بِاسْمِكَ اَللّٰهُمَّ أَحْيَا وَأَمُوتُ.

On the authority of Abu Hurayrah, it is related that the Prophet, upon him be peace, would say:

Whenever any one of you retires to his bed, let him say:

بِاسْمِكَ رَبِّي وَضَعْتُ جَنْبِي، وَبِكَ أَرْفَعُهُ، إِنْ أَمْسَكْتَ نَفْسِي فَارْحَمْهَا، وَإِنْ أَرْسَلْتَهَا فَاحْفَظْهَا بِمَا تَحْفَظُ بِهِ عِبَادَكَ الصَّالِحِينَ.

29

'In Your name, my Lord, I have laid myself down, and in Your name I shall rise. If You take my soul, then have mercy on it; and if You release it, then protect it in the way You protect Your faithful servants.'

That hadith is an excellent commentary on this verse of the Qur'an:

Allah takes the souls at the time of their death, and that which has not died, in its sleep; He withholds that against which He has decreed death, but releases the others til a stated term. (al Zumar 39: 42)

If a believer considers the hadith and the Qur'anic verse together, he will feel that his life, from one moment to the next, is a gift from the hand of the Lord of All the Worlds. It may be that when he lays down for the night, he will rise again only on the Day of Resurrection. In this event, his only request is for mercy. But if he rises to live another day, then his only wish is to live under Allah's protection.

On the authority of al Barra' ibn Azib, it is related that the Prophet, upon him be peace, said:

Whenever you go to your bed, first perform your *wudu'* in the same way that you perform *wudu'* for salah, then lie down on your right side and say:

«اللَّهُمَّ أَسْلَمْتُ نَفْسِي إِلَيْكَ، وَفَوَّضْتُ أَمْرِي إِلَيْكَ، وَأَلْجَأْتُ ظَهْرِي إِلَيْكَ، رَغْبَةً وَرَهْبَةً إِلَيْكَ، لَا مَلْجَأَ وَلَا مَنْجَأَ مِنْكَ إِلَّا إِلَيْكَ، آمَنْتُ بِكِتَابِكَ الَّذِي أَنْزَلْتَ، وَنَبِيِّكَ الَّذِي أَرْسَلْتَ».

'O Allah, I commit myself to Your keeping, and entrust You with my affairs, and fall back on You in longing and in awe. There is no refuge and no escape from You, except with You! I believe in Your Book which You have revealed, and in Your

Prophet whom You have sent.' Then, if you die, you will die in the natural state of faith (*fitrah*).

When the believer closes his eyes and prepares to sleep, he abandons his will for an indeterminate time. Many deliver themselves to the unknown. But the believer commits himself to the keeping of his Lord, and entrusts Him with all his affairs! Undoubtedly, Allah alone is the Protector. In whom, other than Him, can one place one's hope, or trust, to ward off evil or bring about good?

Often what happens when one prepares for sleep is that one's mind remains occupied with thoughts of the day's gain or loss, mistakes made, or successes achieved. One function of the *du'as* which the Prophet taught us is to remove these worries, to enable us through our feelings of awe and longing to reach our resting place at the side of Allah, and to make us, before we drift off to sleep, certain of one thing as we supplicate the Lord: 'I believe in Your Book which You have revealed, and in Your Prophet whom You have sent.' Then, in the comfortable bed of natural faith, the Muslim may rest in peace.

In another hadith it is related that the Prophet, upon him be peace, would say when he went to his bed:

«اللَّهُمَّ رَبَّ السَّمٰوَاتِ وَرَبَّ الْأَرْضِ وَرَبَّ الْعَرْشِ الْعَظِيمِ رَبَّنَا وَرَبَّ كُلِّ شَيْءٍ فَالِقَ الْحَبِّ وَالنَّوَى، مُنْزِلَ التَّوْرَاةِ وَالْإِنْجِيْلِ وَالْقُرْآنِ. . أَعُوْذُ بِكَ مِنْ شَرِّ كُلِّ ذِيْ شَرٍّ. . أَنْتَ آخِذٌ بِنَاصِيَتِهِ. أَنْتَ الْأَوَّلُ فَلَيْسَ قَبْلَكَ شَيْءٌ، وَأَنْتَ الْأَخِرُ فَلَيْسَ بَعْدَكَ شَيْءٌ، وَأَنْتَ الظَّاهِرُ فَلَيْسَ فَوْقَكَ شَيْءٌ، وَأَنْتَ الْبَاطِنُ فَلَيْسَ دُوْنَكَ شَيْءٌ. . . اقْضِ عَنَّا الدَّيْنَ، وَأَغْنِنَا مِنَ الْفَقْرِ».

31

O Allah! Lord of the heavens and Lord of the earth and Lord of the Great Throne! Our Lord and Lord of every thing! Splitter of the grain and date stone! Revealer of the Torah, the Gospels, and Qur'an! I seek refuge in You from the evil of every evil one whose forelock You have seized. You are the First, there is nothing before You, and You are the Last, there is nothing after You. You are the Manifest, there is nothing beyond You, and You are the Concealed, there is nothing before You. Pay our debts for us, and relieve us from poverty.

In another hadith, on the authority of Ali, it is narrated that the Prophet, upon him be peace, would say:

اللَّهُمَّ إِنِّي أَعُوذُ بِوَجْهِكَ الْكَرِيْمِ ، وَكَلِمَاتِكَ التَّامَّةِ مِنْ شَرِّ مَا أَنْتَ آخِذٌ بِنَاصِيَتِهِ، اللَّهُمَّ أَنْتَ تَكْشِفُ الْمَغْرَمَ وَالْمَأْثَمَ . . ، اللَّهُمَّ لَا يُهْزَمُ جُنْدُكَ، وَلَا يُخْلَفُ وَعْدُكَ، وَلَا يَنْفَعُ ذَا الْجَدِّ مِنْكَ الْجَدُّ، سُبْحَانَكَ اَللَّهُمَّ وَبِحَمْدِكَ، .

O Allah, I take refuge in Your kindness from the evil of everything which You have seized by the forelock (everything which comes under Your Power) O Allah, only You remove debt and sin! Your army is never defeated, and Your promise is never broken. The wealth of the wealthy will not protect him from You. Glory be to You, O Allah, and praise!

In another hadith it is related that he would say:

بِاسْمِ اللهِ وَضَعْتُ جَنْبِيْ، اَللَّهُمَّ اغْفِرْ لِي ذَنْبِي، وَأَخْسِيءْ شَيْطَانِيْ، وَفُكَّ رِهَانِي وَثَقِّلْ مِيْزَانِيْ، وَاجْعَلْنِيْ فِي النَّدِيِّ الْأَعْلَى، .

32

In the name of Allah I lay myself down. O Allah, forgive me my wrongdoing, drive away my evil, deliver me of my responsibilities, and place me in one of the highest places in heaven.

In each of the above *du'as* we see the Prophet, upon him be peace, ardently extolling his Lord's greatness. Indeed the *du'as* he used, as he prepared to go to sleep, were and remain inimitable by even the cleverest and most perceptive of masters. In the first part, he gave praise to Perfect Godhood in all of its richness and wide power. Then, after that ardent praise, he summarized the humanity of every true servant of Allah by asking for relief from poverty, debt, sin and the whisperings of the evil one; then by asking for forgiveness and release from every responsibility which binds one to this world . . . because he sought only to be allowed entrance to the highest place in heaven, to the court of the Sublime Companion, *al rafiq al a'la*!

Yet, we must not suppose that the Prophet, upon him be peace, after petitioning his Lord in this manner, simply went off into a deep sleep. By no means! After an hour's rest he was up again to obey the call of his Lord, to renew the recital of His praises in the still of the night, as he had done during the day. Indeed, he had been commanded to do so by the Almighty:

Remember the name of Your Lord in the morning and in the evening, and part of the night bow down before Him, and praise Him a long (time at) night. (al Dahr 76: 25)

The Prophet, alone of all the Muslims, was required to rise for the nightly *tahajjud* prayer. So, whoever prefers to sleep is free to do so. But as for the Prophet, upon him be peace,

Your Lord knows that you keep awake (in prayer) nearly two thirds of the night, or one half it or a third of it, together with some of those who follow you . . . Recite, then, as much of the Qur'an as you may do with ease. (al Muzzammil 73: 20)

33

The biographers of the Prophet record that he used to spend the greater part of every night in prayer and recitation of the Qur'an. It once happened, when the Prophet was in his fifties, that Ibn 'Abbas, then only a youth, was spending the night at the Prophet's house, and when the Prophet, upon him be peace, rose for *tahajjud* prayer, Ibn 'Abbas fell in behind him. Then, as the Prophet continued to recite chapter after chapter from the Qur'an, the boy began to tire until he could wait no longer for the prayer to be over. But the soul of the Prophet, the true worshipper, conquered the effect of his old age so that he was able to continue reciting through the night. Said Ibn 'Abbas: 'I felt like leaving him to pray by himself, and going my own way.'

The Prophet's feet regularly became swollen as a result of these nightly sessions of standing before the Lord of All the Worlds. But the heart borne on the wings of love may cause an aging body to ignore all twinges of pain and experience instead the ecstasy of immersion in the sweetness of worship; as the poet said:

> And when the soul is great, in doing its bidding the body may fall.

But what of the approaching morning? After the still of the night people rise to meet whatever fate awaits them. The words of the Prophet long before the dawn of the new day —

> Glory be to Allah! What trials lie ahead? And what treasures? Awake! You there in the rooms [the Prophet's wives]! For many are the well attired in this world who will be naked in the next.

— prepared for the approaching day with its good and its evil by assembling his household to stand together in prayer.

And who is to say that the coming day will not be the last? 'For many are the well attired in this world who will be naked in the next.' And many are the beggars in this world who will be kings in the next! The next world is the abode of Truth; and before entering it certain preparations must be made.

In another hadith it is related that the Prophet, upon him be peace, sometimes used to say the following *du'a* as he lay down to sleep:

«اَللّٰهُمَّ لَكَ الْحَمْدُ أَنْتَ نُورُ السَّمٰوَاتِ وَالْأَرْضِ وَمَنْ فِيهِنَّ، وَلَكَ الْحَمْدُ أَنْتَ قَيُّومُ السَّمٰوَاتِ وَالْأَرْضِ وَمَنْ فِيهِنَّ، وَلَكَ الْحَمْدُ أَنْتَ رَبُّ السَّمٰوَاتِ وَالْأَرْضِ وَمَنْ فِيهِنَّ، وَلَكَ الْحَمْدُ، أَنْتَ الْحَقُّ، وَوَعْدُكَ الْحَقُّ، وَقَوْلُكَ الْحَقُّ، وَلِقَاؤُكَ حَقٌّ، وَالْجَنَّةُ حَقٌّ وَالنَّارُ حَقٌّ، وَالنَّبِيُّونَ حَقٌّ، وَمُحَمَّدٌ حَقٌّ، وَالسَّاعَةُ حَقٌّ، اَللّٰهُمَّ لَكَ أَسْلَمْتُ وَبِكَ آمَنْتُ، وَعَلَيْكَ تَوَكَّلْتُ، وَإِلَيْكَ أَنَبْتُ، وَبِكَ خَاصَمْتُ، وَإِلَيْكَ حَاكَمْتُ، فَاغْفِرْ لِي مَا قَدَّمْتُ وَمَا أَخَّرْتُ، وَمَا أَسْرَرْتُ وَمَا أَعْلَنْتُ أَنْتَ إِلٰهِي لَا إِلٰهَ إِلَّا أَنْتَ».

O Allah, praise to You! You are the light of the heavens and the earth and all that dwell therein. Praise to You! You are the Lord of the heavens and the earth and all that dwell therein. Praise to You! You are the truth, and Your promise is true, and Your word is true, and Your meeting is true, and the Garden is true, and the Fire is true, and the Prophets were true, and Muhammad is true, and the Hour is true! O Allah, to You I commit myself, and in You I believe and place my trust, and unto You I turn in repentance, and for You I fight, and through You I pass judgment. Forgive me my sins, past and future, open and hidden. You are my God; there is no God but You!

The Prophet would urge his Companions to greet the night in a spirit of purity and virtue by saying:

> Cleanse these bodies of yours, may Allah purify you! For whoever washes before going to sleep will have an angel in his hair for the night saying: 'O Allah, grant him forgiveness for he sleeps in a state of purity.'

Bodily cleanliness is no substitute for purity of soul. Thus, when the Muslim settles into his bed for a night's sleep, his heart should be with Allah, and his tongue occupied with reciting His praises. It is related on the authority of 'Ali that the Prophet, upon him be peace, said to him and his wife Fatimah, may Allah be pleased with them:

> Whenever you go to bed, [or he said] whenever you betake yourselves to bed, recite *Allahu Akbar* (Allah is Great) thirty-three times, and *Subhan Allah* (Glory be to Allah) thirty-three times, and *Al hamdu li Allah* (Praise to Allah) thirty-three times.

In one version of the same hadith they were instructed to repeat *Subhan Allah* thirty-four times. Said 'Ali: 'After hearing this from the Prophet, upon him be peace, I never once neglected to practice it.' When someone asked 'Ali if he did not neglect it on the night of the Battle of Siffin he replied: 'Not even on the eve of Siffin!'

In other words, 'Ali, may Allah be pleased with him, diligently practiced what he had been taught for over thirty years until the fateful battle took place between him and his enemies.

No doubt 'Ali lived a life filled with anxieties; in this world he knew no rest, and it was only when he died that he had his first experience of it. On his tragic death 'A'ishah wrote the following verses:

> So at last he threw down his staff, the toils of his travels now left far behind, like a wanderer in rapture at first sight of home.

But he never allowed his worries to so overwhelm him, as to neglect his nightly recital of what he had learned to recite before going to sleep. Indeed, it is more than likely that the recital helped him overcome, or at least cope with the many worries which beset him.

Among the hadith concerning the Prophet's urging his community to practice regular cleanliness before retiring at night, as well as spiritual purity, is one related on the authority of Abu Umamah:

> I heard the Prophet of Allah say: 'Whoever retires to his bed in a state of purity, and recites the praises of Allah until he is overcome by sleep, will be granted whatever he asks for if he rises during the night to petition Allah for the good of this world or the next.'

In another hadith 'A'ishah said:

> When the Prophet of Allah, peace be upon him, went to his bed, he used to say:

$$
\text{اَللّٰهُمَّ أَمْتِعْنِيْ بِسَمْعِيْ وَبَصَرِيْ، وَاجْعَلْهُمَا الْوَارِثَ}
$$
$$
\text{مِنِّيْ، وَانْصُرْنِيْ عَلٰى عَدُوِّيْ، وَأَرِنِيْ مِنْهُ ثَارِيْ،}
$$
$$
\text{اَللّٰهُمَّ إِنِّيْ أَعُوْذُ بِكَ مِنْ غَلَبَةِ الدَّيْنِ، وَمِنَ الْجُوْعِ}
$$
$$
\text{فَإِنَّهُ بِئْسَ الضَّجِيْعُ،}
$$

> 'O Allah! Allow me to enjoy my hearing and my sight, and make that enjoyment my heir; grant me victory over my enemy, and show me the vengeance I take from him. O Allah, I seek refuge in You from being overcome by defeat, and from hunger; for certainly hunger is a terrible bedfellow.'

In this hadith the Prophet asked Allah to preserve his senses for the rest of his natural life, especially those of sight and hearing, and asked for deliverance from debt and the pangs of hunger.

The Prophet was a human being who sought to live a life of vitality and honor, far removed from self inflicted hardship and suffering. Certainly it is the right of every human being to live such a life. Then let us forget the religious charlatans who would have us welcome suffering and deprivation as if they were things to be cherished; or who would have us believe that religion is some sort of war on well being and dignity.

The *du'a* in the hadith quoted above contains certain words (... grant me victory...) which need to be explained. Before embarking on an explanation, however, there is a question which must be answered first: Did the Prophet harbor any personal enmity for anyone? The answer is, emphatically, no! Where his own rights were concerned the Prophet was an extremely forgiving person. But what provoked him was when the rights of Allah were violated. It was then that the Prophet rose to the defense like an enraged lion. Thus, when the Prophet requested his Lord to give him victory over his enemy, it is as if he was commenting, through his request, on the following verse of the Qur'an:

> And pardon us, and forgive us, and have mercy on us; You are our Master, then give us victory over the people of the disbelievers. (al Baqarah 2: 286)

The disbelievers were a people who left bloody wounds in the very hearts of the believers; the weak among them especially, those who were overpowered and forced to split up, and degraded to such an extent that the wide world restricted them, and seemed no wider than the eye of a needle. It was the right of these poor and oppressed believers to see justice taken from their enemies, and to see the haughtiness of disbelief fallen in the dust. Indeed, this was the very reason for the order to make war against the disbelievers until their power was broken.

> Fight them, and Allah will chastise them at your hands and degrade them; and He will give you victory over them, and bring healing to the breasts of a people who believe, and

remove the rage from within their hearts. (al Tawbah 9: 14
15)

Human nature has certain established characteristics that may not
be effaced or overlooked. There is, however, a kind of muddled religiosity which seeks to do away with reason and to underrate
roundedness of character. Needless to say, Islam has nothing to do
with such religiosity!

Perhaps this hadith, related by 'A'ishah, best indicates the respect
accorded by Islam to human nature. She said:

The Prophet of Allah, upon whom be peace, for as long as I knew
him, never slept without first seeking refuge from cowardice and
indolence, boredom, parsimony, undue pride, embarrassment in
family or financial affairs, the chastisement of the grave, and from
Satan and associating him (with the Almighty).

Thus the Prophet sleeps; but not before making the night come alive
with purity and *dhikr*, so that after no more than an hour of sleep he
awakes for the dawn prayer and prepares to meet another twenty
four hours with the following *du'a*:

$$\text{«أَصْبَحْنَا وَأَصْبَحَ الْمُلْكُ لِلَّهِ، وَالْحَمْدُ لِلَّهِ لَاشَرِيْكَ}$$
$$\text{لَهُ، لَا إِلَهَ إِلَّا هُوَ، وَإِلَيْهِ النُّشُوْرُ».}$$

We have awoken, and the domain belongs to Allah. Praise to
Allah! He has no partner. There is no God but Him; and to
Him is the final issuing.

7

IN THE VASTNESS OF LIFE

Muhammad, upon him be peace, knew Allah and acquainted mankind with Him through his remembrance of Him and through thanksgiving. He drew large numbers of people into the same acts of remembrance and thanksgiving, kindling, whenever necessary, the flames of their ardor and calling them back to the path whenever they strayed. It was he who delivered them from the long night of ignorance so that they might know who their Lord was, and how to live for Him here on earth, and how to prepare for the final return to Him on the day the doors of the heavens will be flung open.

Having a relationship with Allah is more than just spending a few minutes in the morning or evening in making *du'a*, and then going out into the world and doing whatever one pleases. That would make the relationship a fraud. True religion is a person's heeding his Lord in every situation, his keeping his activities within the bounds of what the Lord has commanded and prohibited, acknowledging his human frailties, and seeking the help of the Lord whenever he is beset by difficulties.

The Prophet's life, upon him be peace, was a vivid demonstration of the depth and comprehensiveness of his relationship with Allah. Whether it was a matter of doing or of not doing, nothing in his life ever caused him to be forgetful of Allah. For this reason we find that his *du'as* touch upon so many of the diverse aspects of life, and they are so worded as to harmonize with everything he put his hand to. For example, his charged emotions would cause him to contemplate the first raindrops and say:

41

This rain has only recently been with the Lord.

When some people, on discovering the first fruits of the season had ripened, took them to him, he took one in his hand and said:

«اللَّهُمَّ بَارِكْ لَنَا فِي ثَمَرِنَا، وَبَارِكْ لَنَا فِي مَدِينَتِنَا، وَبَارِكْ لَنَا فِيْ صَاعِنَا، وَبَارِكْ لَنَا فِي مُدِّنَا».

O Allah, bless us in our fruit, and bless us in our settlement, and bless us in our good measure.

Thereafter the Prophet handed the fruit to the youngest children of his Companions present.

Whenever the wind began to blow, he would say:

«اللَّهُمَّ إِنِّي أَسْأَلُكَ خَيْرَهَا، وَخَيْرَ مَا فِيهَا، وَخَيْرَ مَا أَرْسَلْتَ بِهِ، وَأَعُوذُ بِكَ مِنْ شَرِّهَا، وَشَرِّ مَا فِيهَا، وَشَرِّ مَا أَرْسَلْتَ بِهِ»

O Allah, I ask of You the best of it, and the best of what is in it, and the best of what You have sent with it; I seek refuge in You from the evil of it, and from the evil within it, and from the evil You have sent with it.

The Prophet approached whatever came his way with this kind of overflowing spiritual awareness, and applied the teachings of heaven exactly as revealed to him. Let us now examine particular aspects of human society, and the way in which he reformed them in the name, and with the blessings, of Allah.

8

THE FOUNDATION OF
EVERY MUSLIM HOME

The sexual instinct is one that can give rise to serious problems if
subject to sudden outbursts of passion, transgressing the limits set
for it by Allah, or violating the basic human rights of others. If that
is allowed to happen, a person may risk disgrace or even damna-
tion. Indeed, any instinct unchecked by the Shari'ah or Islamic Law
will surely lead to serious trouble.

Allah did not create our instincts so as to oppress or deceive us,
nor so that some people should worship Him by attempting to
suppress or ignore them. On the contrary, He created natural out-
lets for all of our instincts. In the case of our sexual instincts, He
made available to us the institution of marriage and caused love
and mercy to flow from it in order to establish in the home an
atmosphere of tenderness and grace. And He charged His pious
servants to appreciate the value of this felicity, to delight in its
comforts, and not to allow even their eyes to stray beyond its limits. He charged them to direct their energies within marriage to the
bringing up of children, to caring for their future, and to raising a
generation of rightly minded and rightly behaved youth. In the
Qur'an it is written:

> Those who say, 'Our Lord, may our spouses and our off-
> spring be a joy to our eyes and make us leaders of the heed-
> ful'. (al Furqan 25: 74)

The true Muslim is one who shows genuine concern for how his children relate to their Lord and their Muslim brothers and sisters; not one whose only preoccupation is to crowd society with his own undisciplined offspring!

Consider the *du'a* of the Prophet Ibrahim, upon whom be peace.

My Lord, cause me and my offspring to remain constant in prayer, and accept this my prayer. (Ibrahim 14: 40)

To have success in raising children who stand up for the rights of Allah is great prosperity. It is a measure of the magnitude of the faith in the heart of Ibrahim that his dearest wish was to have righteous children. Ordinarily, men wish for children who will become wealthy or powerful or otherwise successfully occupied with the stuff of this world. Beyond that nothing much matters to them. But the Prophets of Allah were of a different mettle, because their concern was with the matter of faith.

You were witnesses that when death presented itself to Ya'qub, he said to his sons: 'Whom will you worship after I am gone?' They said: 'We will worship your God, and the God of your fathers, Ibrahim, Isma'il and Ishaq, the One God; and to Him do we surrender ourselves'. (al Baqarah 2: 133)

The first foundation of the Muslim home is made in the choice (made after seeking the help of Allah) of a good spouse. It is the custom in Islam, a Sunnah (Islamic tradition) that, when husband and wife meet for the first time, the husband should take the name of Allah, place his hand on the forehead of his wife, and say:

May Allah bless each one of us in our partnership.

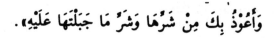

44

'O Allah, I seek from You her good, and the good You created in her; and I seek refuge in You from her evil and the
evil You created in her.

All of us have weaknesses and shortcomings that need to be concealed and forgiven. Anyone who claims to be blessed with a
flawless character is surely self deceived! Furthermore, if man and
wife are truly friends, they must, to preserve their love for one
another, learn to overlook the other's faults and seek help from
Allah.

Among the many distinguishing features of Islam is its association
of the natural human urges with the remembrance of Allah, *dhikr*, so
that the Muslim satisfies, for example, hunger or thirst, in the name
of Allah. So too, in the matter of sexual contact, each partner is
expected to link his or her desire to the name of Allah. The Prophet
of Allah, upon him be peace, said:

If, whenever any one of you makes sexual approach to his or
her mate, you say:

«اللَّهُمَّ جَنِّبْنَا الشَّيْطَانَ وَجَنِّبِ الشَّيْطَانَ مَا رَزَقْتَنَا».

'O Allah, keep Satan away from us, and keep him away from
any offspring You may bless us with', then the Satan will
never harm any offspring you are destined to produce.

Then, in the ordinary course of things, the woman will be subjected
to the labors of child bearing, and the man to the toils of providing
for the family. Quite often the trials will be severe; and in particular
the woman, in the course of pregnancy, childbirth and breast feed-
ing, must undergo great hardship. Through all of this it is best to
turn to Allah and ask for relief and protection from mishap and
harm. The following *du'a* might be proper on such occasions — in
truth, the *du'as* of the Prophet in which he lays bare his heart and
seeks release are so many:

«اَللّٰهُمَّ رَحْمَتَكَ أَرْجُوْ فَلَا تَكِلْنِيْ إِلٰى نَفْسِيْ طَرْفَةَ عَيْنٍ، وَأَصْلِحْ لِيْ شَأْنِيْ كُلَّهُ لَا إِلٰهَ إِلَّا أَنْتَ».

O Allah, have mercy on me! Do not leave me alone for even a moment, and put my affairs in order, there is no God but You.

«يَاحَيُّ يَاقَيُّوْمُ بِرَحْمَتِكَ أَسْتَغِيْثُ».

O Living, O Eternal One! I beseech You for Your Mercy!

لَا إِلٰهَ إِلَّا أَنْتَ سُبْحَانَكَ إِنِّيْ كُنْتُ مِنَ الظَّالِمِيْنَ».

There is no God but You, Glory to You, I have been among those who wrong themselves.

The subject of relations between the sexes is one that deserves further explanation.

According to some Christians, the highest piety is the severance of these relations, and the turning of a deaf ear, by good men and women, to the call of the hated sexual instinct. Monasticism was raised, and still stands, on this unnatural foundation. But if we look more closely, we see that some people are possessed of a naturally weak sexual instinct so that abstention has little meaning for them, while others are possessed of strong instincts so that they must either resort to satisfying their desires illegitimately or to a vicious battle with those instincts which rarely, if ever, leaves them physically or psychologically unscarred. To say that a person has attained true piety in either of these cases is unacceptable.

Islam, by contrast, in addition to making marriage lawful, and within the compass of every adult Muslim has also declared it to be an act of worship.

It is quite a perversity, then, that the "modern" world[1] should seek to confuse the issue by mocking Islamic teachings on the subject; particularly when we consider that the modern world has a very confused set of values on sexual relationships. The number of illegitimate children born each year in so-called modern society is almost as great as, in some countries, the number of legitimate births. Wandering from one sexual partner to another is commonplace.

According to the widow of the former American President, John F. Kennedy, her husband had sexual relations with over a hundred women. Even more than those in power, the playboys of the world are able to thieve the honor of women by the hundreds! Is it not more than a little absurd that making what amounts to a small multitude of sexual conquests is normal or socially acceptable, while the teachings of Islam in regard to the family are condemned as reactionary and retrogressive?

Among men esteemed in the West as their greatest and most popular political figures are many whose promiscuity is well known. Despite this, they continue to enjoy general respect and admiration. The well known Egyptian author, Anis Mansur, writes:

> It comes as no surprise that a book on the life of the tiger of French politics, Georges Clemenceau (1841-1929) should have been released in France. Indeed the man entered the century's most frightful political battles and managed to emerge victorious from them all. Furthermore, his ability to speak simultaneously to twenty different people on twenty different subjects is well known. But who could have imagined that the same man had over eight hundred lovers, and more than forty bastard sons!

---

[1] I have taken some liberties here with the original in which the author speaks of the Western world. In fact, however, it is not the West, per se, that is troubling, but modernity and post-modernity and the secular attitudes and approaches that these are based upon. Thus the same sorts of twisted attitudes toward Islam flourish today in many of our Eastern Muslim societies. Translator.

But when Clemenceau discovered that his American wife had been unfaithful to him, he opened the door in the middle of the night and threw her out on the street dressed in nothing but a nightgown!

I cannot help but be shocked by this striking example of what is called the 'double standard.' Mansur goes on to say:

Clemenceau, like any other human predator, had almost no respect for women. No one has ever said anything worse about women than what he said about them.

Yet, Western leaders (the French Deputy Minister of Defense has eulogized him in a book) still number him among their greatest men! Why? Because he was an adulterer for whom the institution of marriage meant nothing? Is adultery such a trifling matter! Such is the traditional Western attitude, created and nurtured by the Crusades, and now exported to the East by the same people.

Islam has elevated the meaning of marriage to heights deserving of every acclaim. Marriage is not an institution by means of which a man is entitled to full control over the life of a woman! On the contrary, it is a free contract, beginning and ending with the permission of Allah and with His guarantee. In his famous address at the 'Farewell Pilgrimage' the Prophet of Allah, upon him be peace, said:

And heed Allah in the matter of women; for of a certainty you take them in the trust of Allah, and you enjoy their persons in the Word of Allah!

The Islamic marriage contract is, by its nature, material and spiritual, worldly and other worldly, so that the home which is established through it will thrive with tranquillity, love and mercy between the partners. Marriage also has a social dimension, by means of which human development is sustained in purity and divine guidance.

The Qur'an refers to these natural elements of marriage as 'Rights of Allah', for He wants the home's foundations to be righteousness, heedfulness, and unselfish sharing of all life's responsibilities. The marriage *khutbah* shows Islam's high esteem for marriage. Scholars say it is best to recite a brief and befitting *khutbah* at the time of marriage. The best example is related by 'Abd Allah ibn Mas'ud:

The Prophet of Allah, upon whom be peace, taught us the following *khutbah*:

«الْحَمْدُ لِلهِ، نَحْمَدُهُ وَنَسْتَعِينُهُ، وَنَسْتَغْفِرُهُ، وَنَعُوذُ بِهِ مِنْ شُرُورِ أَنْفُسِنَا، مَنْ يَهْدِ اللهُ فَلاَ مُضِلَّ لَهُ، وَمَنْ يُضْلِلْ فَلاَ هَادِيَ لَهُ، وَأَشْهَدُ أَن لاَّ إِلَهَ إِلاَّ اللهُ وَحْدَهُ لاَ شَرِيْكَ لَهُ، وَأَشْهَدُ أَنَّ مُحَمَّداً عَبْدُهُ وَرَسُولُهُ، أَرْسَلَهُ بِالْحَقِّ بَشِيْراً وَنَذِيْراً بَيْنَ يَدَيِ السَّاعَةِ، مَنْ يُطِعِ اللهَ وَرَسُولَهُ فَقَدْ رَشَدَ، وَمَنْ يَعْصِهِمَا فَإِنَّهُ لاَ يَضُرُّ إِلاَّ نَفْسَهُ وَلاَ يَضُرُّ اللهَ شَيْئاً».

«يَاأَيُّهَا النَّاسُ اتَّقُوا رَبَّكُمُ الَّذِي خَلَقَكُمْ مِنْ نَفْسٍ وَاحِدَةٍ وَخَلَقَ مِنْهَا زَوْجَهَا وَبَثَّ مِنْهُمَا رِجَالاً كَثِيْراً وَنِسَاءً وَاتَّقُوا اللهَ الَّذِي تَسَاءَلُونَ بِهِ وَالأَرْحَامَ إِنَّ اللهَ كَانَ عَلَيْكُمْ رَقِيْباً».

«يَاأَيُّهَا الَّذِيْنَ آمَنُوا اتَّقُوا اللهَ حَقَّ تُقَاتِهِ وَلاَ تَمُوتُنَّ إِلاَّ وَأَنْتُم مُّسْلِمُونَ».

«يَاأَيُّهَا الَّذِيْنَ آمَنُوا اتَّقُوا اللهَ وَقُوْلُوا قَوْلاً سَدِيْداً. يُصْلِحْ لَكُمْ أَعْمَالَكُمْ وَيَغْفِرْ لَكُمْ ذُنُوبَكُمْ، وَمَنْ يُطِعِ اللهَ وَرَسُولَهُ فَقَدْ فَازَ فَوْزاً عَظِيْماً».

'Praise to Allah! We praise Him and seek His help! We seek His forgiveness and in Him seek refuge from the evil within ourselves! Whoever Allah guides will not be led astray by anyone; and whosoever Allah leads astray will not be guided by anyone! I give witness that there is no god but Allah, who is One and has no partner. And I give witness that Muhammad is His slave and His Prophet whom He sent with the truth as a giver of good tidings and as a warner before the coming of the Hour! Whosoever obeys Allah and His Prophet will be rightly guided. But whosoever disobeys them will bring harm only to himself, and will bring no harm to Allah.'

O mankind, heed your Lord, who created you from a single soul, and created from it its mate, then caused to issue forth from them many men and women. Heed Allah in whose name you seek your rights from one another, and (take heed that you do not violate the rights of your) relations; surely Allah ever watches over you. (al Nisa' 4: 1)

O you who believe, heed Allah as He should be heeded and do not allow death to overtake you before you have surrendered yourselves to Him. (Al 'Imran 3: 102)

O you who believe, heed Allah, and speak the truth, He will set right your deeds for you and forgive you your sins. Whosoever obeys Allah and His Prophet has succeeded with a great success. (al Ahzab 33: 70-71)

Thereafter, when the *khutbah* has been completed, the contract may be solemnized and the marriage partners reminded to heed Allah, to live together in harmony, and remain within the limits set for them by Allah.

The verses cited in the marriage *khutbah* are an excellent introduction to married life. They direct the Muslim's attention toward founding a family which will contribute to the strength of Islam and the community. Indeed, marriage is a contract with very far reaching consequences. As the years pass and the couple become parents devoted to the upbringing of a new generation, the family develops and grows in number. Then, as the age of the two parents increases, the children mature and set out on their own. But how will the younger generation treat those who went before them? In the Qur'an it is written:

We have counseled man that he show kindness to his parents; his mother carried him painfully, and painfully she gave birth to him; his bearing and his weaning may take thirty months. Then, when he is fully grown, and reaches forty years, he says, 'O my Lord, inspire me to be thankful for Your blessings wherewith You have blessed me and my parents, and to do good by which You will be pleased; and make my children to do right by me. I have turned to You in repentance: for, verily, I am one of those who have surrendered themselves to You'. (al Ahqaf 46: 15)

And so the present generation should celebrate the praises of the Great Creator, gratefully remembering the favors bestowed by Him on the preceding generation and constantly urging Him to bestow His bounty and mercy on the coming generation. This is the function of the Muslim home; the home in which the relationship between the Lord and mankind is zealously preserved through diligent observance of all forms of regular worship. Small wonder, then, that the angels at the throne of Allah should pray for those who inhabit such homes:

Our Lord! You encompass everything in mercy and knowledge, therefore, forgive those who repent and follow Your way, and guard them against the chastisement of the Fire. Our Lord! and admit them to the Gardens of Eden that You promised them and those who are righteous of their fathers, their wives, and their children. Surely You are the All Mighty and All Wise. (al Mu'min 40: 7)

We shall see how the first Muslim home, the home of the Prophet of Allah, upon him be peace, and those who inhabited it, the wives of the Prophet, was the best example for all who live to seek the next world, and to draw nearer to Allah in truth. It was not a place of ease and luxury, but of constant *dhikr* and Qur'anic recitation, of standing long in prayer at night, and of praise for Allah. In sum, then, the Muslim home constitutes the single most important factor in the proper upbringing and orientation of the new generation. The preservation of this institution is then a guarantee of uprightness in faith.

9

EARNING A LIVING

The Muslim leaves his home to attend to the duties he is required
to perform; the professional man or civil servant to his office, the
laborer to his factory, the merchant to his store, the farmer to his
fields. Generally, when people set out for their daily work they are
weighed down by the anxieties of having to earn a living. Indeed,
some want ever more for themselves and for their families, regardless of whether they be rich or poor. The desires of a lifetime never
stand still, and the energy spent in realizing them eventually
drains the individual of all inward resources. Indeed, it is hard to
calculate the human energy expended in this single pursuit.

It may be that the Prophet too, upon him be peace, had this in mind,
for whenever he left his house, he never failed to recite this *du'a*:

بِاسْمِ اللهِ، تَوَكَّلْتُ عَلَى اللهِ، اَللّٰهُمَّ إِنِّي أَعُوذُ بِكَ
مِنْ أَنْ أَزِلَّ أَوْ أُزَلَّ، أَوْ أَضِلَّ أَوْ أُضَلَّ، أَوْ أَظْلِمَ أَوْ
أُظْلَمَ، أَوْ أَجْهَلَ أَوْ يُجْهَلَ عَلَيَّ. . . .»

In the name of Allah (I go out); I place my trust in Allah! O
Allah, I seek refuge in You from being made to stumble,
from straying and from being made to stray, from doing
wrong to others and from being wronged by others, and
from losing my temper with others, and their losing it with
me.

The Prophet did not seek supremacy over anyone else; he wanted only to avoid falling into error or causing someone else to fall into it. He wanted guidance for himself and for others, he sought Allah's protection so that he might not misunderstand the intentions of someone else and so that he might not have his own intentions misinterpreted by one who might cause him harm, and he disliked every form of wrongdoing. These were the matters he uttered before his Lord, and for which he sought His help.

It was the Prophet's wish, upon him be peace, that every Muslim should bind himself to the Lord before leaving the house to attend to the day's affairs.

Anas related that the Prophet, upon him be peace, said:

Whoever says when leaving home,

«بِسْمِ اللَّهِ، تَوَكَّلْتُ عَلَى اللَّهِ، وَلاَ حَوْلَ وَلاَ قُوَّةَ إِلَّا بِاللَّهِ».

'In the name of Allah; I place my trust in Allah, there is no power and no strength save in Allah', will have it said to him or her (as if in answer), 'You will be guided, you will be provided for, and you will be protected.'

Normally, close contact with others will cause some problems to arise. Sometimes, a little friction will generate great evil. Further, no amount of mental awareness — regardless of how finely tuned it may be — can obviate one's need for Allah's protection. He is the safeguard, may His name be praised, of all those who put their faith in Him, and seek shelter in Him. No Muslim should ever rely exclusively on his own resources. Rather he should ever seek to draw the support of the Almighty, saying, as the Prophet taught him to say:

«اَللَّهُمَّ لَا سَهْلَ إِلَّا مَا جَعَلْتَهُ سَهْلًا، وَأَنْتَ إِذَا شِئْتَ تَجْعَلُ الْحَزْنَ سَهْلًا».

O Allah, nothing is easy except that which You make easy;
and, when You will, You can make any difficulty easy.

In times of hardship and anxiety the Muslim's attachment to his
Lord naturally grows more tenacious. On the authority of Ibn 'Umar
it is related that the Prophet, upon him be peace, said:

What is there to stop any of you, when you are visited by
hard times, from saying whenever you go out from your
homes:

بِسْمِ اللهِ عَلَى نَفْسِيْ وَمَالِي وَدِيْنِي، اَللّٰهُمَّ رَضِّنِي
بِقَضَائِكَ، وَبَارِكْ فِيَا قُدِّرَ لِيْ، حَتَّى لَا أُحِبَّ تَعْجِيْلَ
مَا أَخَّرْتَ، وَلَا تَأْخِيْرَ مَا عَجَّلْتَ».

'In the name of Allah for myself, my wealth, and my religion. O Allah, make me happy with what You decide for me,
and bless me in whatever You decide for me so that I desire
neither the expediting of what You have postponed, nor the
postponement of what You have expedited!

Praise be to Allah! The Prophet's understanding of the human condition was truly profound. Into what limitless storehouse of faith
did he delve to steady and preserve the relationships that all those
who came to him had with Allah? It is related on the authority of
Barra' ibn Azib that a man complained to the Prophet of feeling
alienated. The Prophet asked him to repeat the following very often:

سُبْحَانَ الْمَلِكِ الْقُدُّوْسِ، رَبُّ الْمَلَائِكَةِ وَالرُّوحِ،
جَلَّلْتَ السَّمٰوَاتِ وَالْأَرْضَ بِالْعِزَّةِ وَالْجَبَرُوْتِ».

Glory to the Holy Monarch, Lord of the Angels and the Soul!
You honor the heavens and the earth with Your Power and
Glory!

Barra' further reports that when the man repeated these words, the feeling left him. He must have been a sensitive soul inclined toward solitude and away from company. Life is not something that reassures or even pleases such people, and they generally fear it despite their need to partake in it. This man complained to the Prophet of his persistent feeling of alienation, and the Prophet advised him to repeat the *du'a* which urged the man to intimacy with Allah.

But, of course, the Prophet neither liked to see solitude become a weakness, nor to see the practice of constant *dhikr* used as a cover for a certain sort of psychological inadequacy.

It is related on the authority of 'Awf ibn Malik that once, when the Prophet had decided a legal case between two men, the one ruled against turned away and said: 'Allah suffices for me and He is the most Trustworthy.' Upon which the Prophet said: 'Allah reproaches people for their weakness. You should be more astute (intelligent, firm, patient) so that if ever you are really overcome by something, you may say, "Allah suffices me, and He is the most Trustworthy".'

The loser's state of mind did not escape the Prophet's notice or understanding. In truth, the man, overcome by his defeat, had sought only to hide his disappointment by saying, 'Allah suffices for me and He is the most Trustworthy.' The words, used thus, could be described as words of truth intended to convey a falsehood.

By contrast, when the Muslims who lost the Battle of Uhud uttered these words, as they rose the next morning, dressed their wounds, and threw themselves into preparations to avenge their defeat at the hands of the Makkan idolaters, they did not do so out of weakness. When it was said to them:

All the people have gathered against you. (Al 'Imran 3: 173)

They replied,

Allah suffices for us and He is the most Trustworthy. (Al 'Imran 3: 173)

So used, the *du'a* bears its true and accepted meaning.

It is not permissible to say these words in mere acceptance of the status quo, while standing idly by awaiting a miracle to somehow do what one is unable, or unwilling, to do for oneself. There is no securing the aid of heaven without endeavor, no realizing hopes without expending effort. That is why the Khalifah 'Umar said,

> Let no one who desists from working for his daily bread say, 'O Allah, give me my daily bread', when he is old enough to know that gold and silver do not fall as rain from the sky.

It is true that in our times this can be at best a very rare complaint that people voice trust in God and then do nothing. The trouble with the modern world is rather the great number of people who do things but without trusting in God. Everywhere people leave their houses in the morning in busy quest of one precious thing or another; and if the opportunity should arise to grab some new valuable, their mouths instantly begin to water again. Thus they eat without ever satisfying their appetites. Trapped in this fervent delirium the heart has no desire but for ever more acquisitions.

But should a person turn away from this decline, should his finer senses function again so that he can distinguish the face of the Almighty through the heaped and folded mists of worldly desire, and then remember His name, and His revelation, and take hold of His verses and teachings, then what would be his reward? The Prophet, upon him be peace, said:

Whoever goes into the marketplace and says,

«لاَ إِلَهَ إِلاَّ اللَّهُ، وَحْدَهُ لاَ شَرِيْكَ لَهُ، لَهُ الْمُلْكُ، وَلَهُ الْحَمْدُ، يُحْيِي وَيُمِيْتُ، وَهُوَ حَيٌّ لاَ يَمُوْتُ، بِيَدِهِ الْخَيْرُ، وَهُوَ عَلَى كُلِّ شَيْءٍ قَدِيْرٌ».

'There is no God but Allah, He is one and has no partner, His is the Glory and His is the praise, Giver of life and death; He is the Living who does not die. In His hand is all good, and He is Powerful over everything,' that man will have a thousand thousand good deeds credited to him, and a thousand thousand bad deeds erased, and he will be elevated a thousand thousand ranks.

Such a huge reward will not be attained by the mere utterance of a few words, but by those who achieve a state of certainty regarding the presence of the Almighty and His beneficence, so that they rely on the One in whose Hand is all Goodness without ever having to resort to cunning or deception. The scholars of Islam have emphatically stated that such great rewards are never promised in return for insignificant deeds or faltering resolutions.

In the matter of earning a living for one's self and one's family, good and bad may often become confused. However, the true Muslim realizes that a soul nourished on ill-gotten gains will never be admitted to Paradise, and that since Allah is Himself Pure, He will accept only those who are themselves pure. Therefore, it is essential that the Muslim should exercise caution in all his dealings. The Prophet, upon him be peace, taught us to use the following *du'as*:

اللَّهُمَّ اكْفِنِي بِحَلَالِكَ عَنْ حَرَامِكَ، وَأَغْنِنِي بِفَضْلِكَ عَمَّنْ سِوَاكَ».

O Allah, suffice me with Your *halal* (lawful) from seeking Your *haram* (unlawful), and free me by Your beneficence from seeking the help of others.

«اللَّهُمَّ إِنِّي أَسْأَلُكَ عِلْماً نَافِعاً، وَرِزْقاً طَيِّباً، وَعَمَلاً مُتَقَبَّلاً».

O Allah, I ask You for knowledge that is useful, sustenance that is pure and deeds that are accepted.

The world's nature is such that one sometimes finds himself in a situation where he could be corrupted, or where the ignorance of people tempt him to behave foolishly toward them, or to seek revenge on them. It is far better, however, that he leave his home each morning prepared to tolerate and forbear. Anas ibn Malik related that the Prophet, upon him be peace, once asked his Companions:

'Are you unable to follow the example of Abu Damdam?' They said, 'Who is Abu Damdam?' The Prophet replied, 'Every morning he used to say,

«اللَّهُمَّ إِنِّيْ قَدْ وَهَبْتُ نَفْسِيْ وَعِرْضِيْ لَكَ» .

"O Allah, I make a gift to You of my life and my honor", so that he never cursed anyone who cursed him, or wronged anyone who wronged him, or molested anyone who molested him.'

This world is indeed full of things that stir up individual men and women, even whole communities. Involvement in them stems from deep within the human personality. Let us then consider the attitude of the Prophets with regard to these matters, as a sort of prelude to the position of the Prophet Muhammad, upon him be peace.

The Prophets were human beings like ourselves, their elevated positions in no way exempted them from the same sort of trials and tribulations, the same duties and responsibilities. Rather, the truth of the matter is that their trials and tribulations were far more severe than those suffered by ordinary men.

The Prophet Yusuf, like any other man, hated prison and longed for his freedom, and so he said to his about-to-be-released cell mate, 'Remember me to your master, the King.' And why shouldn't he have asked this favor? Yusuf was innocent, and wrongly imprisoned. And since his cell mate knew him to be a good and righteous man, why shouldn't he speak of Yusuf with his master, the King?

But Allah willed that the cell mate should forget Yusuf, who then remained in prison for a number of years.

The fated day arrived, however, and the King sent for Yusuf. But by that time Yusuf had attained such self reliance and maturity that he hesitated before answering the King's call, and demanded that first the King should recognize his position as a man wrongly accused and imprisoned. Only then did Yusuf agree to leave prison and, thereafter, take on the task of overseeing the wealth of Egypt.

The Prophet Musa too was a man, like any other, in no way immune to the sting of loneliness when he found himself a fugitive in the land of Madyan. After drawing water for two girls, he retreated to the shade of a tree and called to his Lord:

> O Lord! Surely I have need of whatever good You might send down upon me. (al Qasas 28: 24)

At last help did come to him when he found the refuge he had been seeking with the headman of Madyan, who said to him:

> You have escaped from a wicked people. (al Qasas 28: 25)

Then Musa married the headman's daughter, and lived there with them in preparation for his divine mission. And the Prophet Lut was a man, like any other, when he felt distressed at the way the wrong-doers from among his people cast lascivious glances toward the angels who had come to visit him. Indeed, he wished that he had the power to somehow teach those wrongdoers a lesson; until the angels assured him that the end was near for them.

> Early in the morning there came upon them a lasting punishment: 'Taste, then, the suffering which I inflict when My warnings are disregarded!' (al Qamar 54: 38-9)

The comments of the Last Prophet, upon him be peace, concerning certain of the stories we have related above reveal an interesting aspect of his personality. Concerning Lut, he said, 'Allah had mercy upon Lut; for he sought refuge in Him alone.'

In other words, Allah had no intention of deserting Lut, just as Lut had no real regrets over his own inability to teach a lesson to his people.

As a matter of fact, Muhammad's perception of the Almighty and His support was without equal. The Prophet was called 'the Trusting' for this very reason. It was his extraordinary sense of total reliance upon Allah that gave strength to his call to faith, and to the propagation of his message, in an entirely hostile world. The first person to threaten him and attempt to shout him down was his own uncle, Abu Lahab. So there would never have been the remotest chance of success for the nascent call had it not been for the faith and confidence of Muhammad in his Lord.

The Prophet's comments on the story of Lut imply strength and confidence as against his comments on the story of Yusuf which imply humility and pride. The Prophet said: 'If I had been in prison for as long a time as Yusuf, I would have answered the King's summons right away.' In other words, he would have sought immediate release from prison without waiting for his innocence to be established through the questioning of the women and their well known answer. Here, the Prophet, upon him be peace, with obvious modesty, allows his human nature to express its longing after freedom, and its dislike for restraint and confinement.

Therefore, the Prophets, though able to overcome the natural susceptibilities that stir the common man, had no assurance, when they plunged headlong into battle, that they would survive, or when they spent of their wealth, that they would never find themselves in want. Indeed, their exemplary characters required them to pay the price of greatness, just like anyone else. It only remains to state that the Prophets lived on a pinnacle from which they were never allowed to descend. The position they occupied was the purest and the most elevated position ever held by man.

Let us now turn to the nature of the relationship that the Prophet Muhammad had with the material world; was he attracted by it, or was he above it? The answer is that he knew the world for what it is, tasting of it in a healthy, unaffected manner, while occupying himself at the same time with what is greater and more noble. He was absorbed by the majesty of the Almighty; his greatest satisfaction was in performing salah, and his soul found in fasting its natural feeding-place.

The Prophet required his wives to adopt the same sort of approach to the world that he had, explaining to them that there was no place in his house for the seekers of the things of this world:

> If you desire the worldly life and its attractions, then come, I will make you provision, and set you free with kindliness. (al Ahzab 33: 28)

His wives did occupy themselves as he desired, sparing little effort to attain his level of worship and *dhikr* and drawing near to Allah. It is related on the authority of Juwayriyah, may Allah be pleased with her, that once the Prophet, upon him be peace, left her in her place of prayer when he went out for morning prayer at the mosque. When he returned sometime before noon, he found her in the same position, and asked:

> Have you been in the same position all day long? She replied 'Yes'. Then the Prophet, upon him be peace, said: 'After leaving you I repeated one sentence three times. If those words were placed on the scales, they would outweigh all that you have done today.

$$ \text{«سُبْحَانَ اللهِ وَبِحَمْدِهِ، عَدَدَ خَلْقِهِ، وَرِضَا نَفْسِهِ،} $$
$$ \text{وَزِنَةَ عَرْشِهِ، وَمِدَادَ كَلِمَاتِهِ».} $$

"Glory be to Allah, and praise Him, in the expanse of His creation, as much as He pleases, as much as the weight of

His throne, and as much as the ink it would take to record all His words".'

On the authority of Abu Hurayrah it is related that the Prophet said:

For me to say,

«سُبْحَانَ اللّٰهِ، وَالْحَمْدُ لِلّٰهِ، وَ لَا إِلٰهَ إِلَّا اللّٰهُ، وَاللّٰهُ أَكْبَرُ».

'Glory to Allah, Praise to Allah, There is no god except Allah, and Allah is the Greatest', is more dear to me than every-thing under the sun.

His happiness in repeating these words and weighing their mean-ing was more appealing to him than possession of everything the world had to offer. And even if he had had tons of gold and silver, what would he have done with them? He himself once said that if he had a mountain of gold, he would spend it all on the needs of the poor before three nights and days had passed; if anything remained he would keep it in reserve against times of famine and pestilence.

No, his love was for something else; for Allah, for His Book, for His pleasure, for exchange with Him. His feelings for the Qur'an, the Prophet expressed thus:

«اَللّٰهُمَّ أَنَا عَبْدُكَ، وَابْنُ عَبْدِكَ، وَابْنُ أَمَتِكَ، وَفِي قَبْضَتِكَ، نَاصِيَتِي بِيَدِكَ، مَاضٍ فِيَّ حُكْمُكَ، عَدْلٌ فِيَّ قَضَاؤُكَ أَسْأَلُكَ بِكُلِّ اسْمٍ هُوَ لَكَ، سَمَّيْتَ بِه نَفْسَكَ، أَوْ أَنْزَلْتَهُ فِي كِتَابِكَ، أَوْ عَلَّمْتَهُ أَحَدًا مِنْ خَلْقِكَ، أَوِ اسْتَأْثَرْتَ بِه فِي مَكْنُونِ الْغَيْبِ عِنْدَكَ، أَنْ تَجْعَلَ الْقُرْآنَ الْكَرِيمَ رَبِيعَ قَلْبِي، وَضِيَاءَ بَصَرِي، وَذَهَابَ حُزْنِي، وَجَلَاءَ هَمِّي وَغَمِّي».

63

O Allah, I am Your servant, the son of Your servant, the son of Your maid servant, and entirely at Your service. You hold me by my forelock. Your decree is what controls me, and Your commands to me are just. I beseech You by every one of Your names, those which You use to refer to Yourself, or have revealed in Your Book, or have taught to any one of Your creation, or have chosen to keep hidden with You in the Unseen, to make al Qur'an al Karim the springtime of my heart, the light of my eyes, the departure of my grief, and the vanishing of my affliction and my sorrow.

When his life's foundation was Divine Revelation (*wahy*), how could it not also be his constant companion? At home and abroad, Revelation was with him in his prayers, and in the very fabric of his consciousness. It is related that the Prophet, upon him be peace, once asked his close companion, 'Abd Allah ibn Mas'ud, to recite the Qur'an for him.

'Abd Allah said: 'Me? Read it to you? And it is you to whom it is revealed!' The Prophet said: 'It is just that I would love to hear it from someone else.' So 'Abd Allah began reciting from the beginning of the Surah entitled 'Women', until he reached the following verse:

How then shall it be, when We bring forward from every nation a witness, and bring you forward as a witness to the witnesses? (al Nisa 4: 41)

He glanced up to see the Prophet's eyes filled with tears, and then the Prophet said, 'Enough!'

Sometimes the Prophet, upon him be peace, would fast on consecutive days without breaking his fast in the evening. When some of his Companions attempted to do the same, he forbade them, saying:

You are not the same as me. I spend the night with my Lord, and He gives me sustenance.

We can explain this by saying that his utter devotion to Allah had brought about a physical change in the Prophet so that he was able to drastically reduce the amount of food and sleep he needed each day and night. Yet, in spite of his overwhelming spiritual authority, he was a man among men, familiar with their natures, and awake to their problems. He lived in this world in the name of Allah, and never strayed a hair's breadth from the straight path.

It is inconceivable that we too could achieve the same relationship with the material world. We are neither able nor required to do so. Certain ascetics have attempted to quarrel with the world, living on its fringes, and emulating (in their own estimation) the elevated lives of the Prophets of Allah. But what a difference!

No make up can ever reproduce the redness of a true blush. And artificial flowers, while they may resemble the real thing and last longer, have nothing of a true flower's sap of life, or delicacy, or fragrance. If a man sleeps on a reed mat so that he awakes with the imprint of it clearly visible on his skin, has he thereby successfully emulated the way of life of a Prophet? One who never gave the world more than a vacant stare because his heart was in constant communion with his Lord, awake in His presence, absorbed in His contemplation? A man does not become a general because he wears a general's uniform.

The position of man with regard to the material world was explained for us by the Prophet of Allah, upon him be peace. Let it suffice as eminence enough for any man to live his life as one who has truly aspired to this position.

Qarun was a man of great material wealth. Those who loved the world would look at him in envy and say: 'If only we had as much as Qarun!' Now Allah never required that Qarun should abandon his wealth. The demands He did make of him can be counted on the fingers of one hand. 'Who made you wealthy when you could have been a beggar?' Certainly it was Allah. Then look at your wealth and say: 'It is the will of Allah! There is no power except in Allah.' But the man (Qarun) was deluded, so he said, 'My genius is the secret of my wealth.'

Let us accept, for argument's sake, that his genius was the reason for his wealth. But then who, in his estimation, gave him the gift of genius? Certainly it was Allah. But the careless are ever unmindful. When Allah gives something to someone He expects that His gift be acknowledged. Is there anything difficult in that? Then, He expects those who take of His bounty to be merciful and not severe, just and not tyrannical, upright and not corrupt. Allah said, Exalted is He:

> Seek, amidst that which Allah has given you, the Last Abode and forget not your portion of the present world; and do good, as Allah has been good to you, and seek not to work corruption in the earth. (al Qasas 28: 77)

Unfortunately, however, so many of those to whom Allah has given material wealth think only of themselves and never of others; rather, they multiply their own wealth at the expense of the poor:

> O believers! Let not your wealth nor your children distract you from remembrance of Allah; whoever does that, they will be the Losers. And spend of what We have provided you before death comes to one of you and he says, 'O Lord, if only You would grant me a delay for a short while so that I may spend and become one of the righteous!' (al Muna-fiqun 63: 9-10)

The Prophet, upon him be peace, constantly urged his Companions to spend whatever they could on those less fortunate than themselves. Miserliness was intolerable to him.

The new agnostic philosophies which have managed to sweep the modern masses off their feet were founded in circumstances of extreme niggardliness, harshness and blind selfishness. It is related on the authority of Abu Hurayrah that the Prophet, upon him be peace, said:

Not a morning passes in which the servants of Allah arise but that two angels descend; one of whom says: 'O Allah, give increase to those who spend', while the other says, 'O Allah, destroy those who withhold.'

And he taught that Allah says:

O My servant! I spend and spend on you. But the hand of Allah is ever full, its bounty undiminishing throughout the day and night. Can you imagine how much I have spent since I created the heavens and earth? Still, what I hold in my Hand has not decreased.

The Prophet also made it explicit that only that wealth which was come by honestly can be accepted as legitimate expenditure in His way. Allah required all Prophets in particular, and humankind in general, to seek to earn their living by *halal* means only:

O Prophets, partake of the wholesome things, and do right-eousness. (al Mu'minun 23: 51)

and:

You who believe, eat any wholesome things we have provided you with, and thank Allah, if it is Him that you serve. (al Baqarah 2: 172)

In the light of these teachings a whole generation developed amongst whom the rich cared for the underprivileged, shunned the worship of wealth, and refused all doubtful dealings.

The shining example of the Prophet, upon him be peace, has always been an inspiration to the society to which that generation gave rise. The Prophet, in relation to the world and its wealth, showed gratitude in times of affluence and patience in times of poverty. And he was indeed a wealthy man.

He found you destitute and made you rich. (al Duha 93: 8)

His wealth came, in his youth, from his successful management of the commercial affairs of his wife, Khadijah. Later on, his position as Commander in Chief entitled him to a fifth share of the spoils of war, which were considerable even at that early date in the history of Muslim conquests.

Yet he never took personal possession of any of that wealth. He would always distribute his wealth among the needy. Sometimes his constant generosity, and that of his righteous wives, would exhaust all of his income, so that when they awoke the next morning there remained nothing even for their breakfast.

One of the better-known incidents of the Prophet's life, upon him be peace, is how he was unable to take rest during his final illness until assured that the little bit of gold he had in his house had been distributed among the poor. 'How can I meet my Lord when I still have this in my possession?', he rhetorically asked his Companions.

It is also well known that his possessions were not to be inherited by his family. Everything was distributed in the way of Allah. The Prophet used to say this prayer:

O Allah, grant the family of Muhammad sufficient provision.

When he made his choice in favor of The Sublime Companion,[1] he resembled the inhabitants of Heaven, even before he reached there, so aloof had he become from the world and its attractions.

---

[1] During his final illness, the Prophet was visited by an angel who gave him a choice between restoration to health and the companionship of the Almighty.

10

ON A JOURNEY AND ON RETURN

To facilitate travel, tremendous projects have been undertaken the world over, and people make journeys more and more often, for diverse purposes, social and material. Yet, for all the progress and innovation, parting from home and loved ones, exposing oneself to changes in daily routine and dietary habits, the risk of the journey itself, fear of accident, uncertainty of how it may turn out; all of these things contribute to making travel a source of concern in the life of any human being.

The Prophet of Allah, upon him be peace, traveled many times in his early youth, during his management of Khadijah's trade, and then during his prophetic mission. He thus had a very true understanding of the traveler's feelings and anxieties. In his *du'as* and *dhikr* he shows the most sensitive perception of the traveler's need for company and solace, and in sublime words answers that need. He said:

> Let whoever intends to set out on a journey say to those he leaves behind:

$$ \text{»أَسْتَوْدِعُكُمُ اللَّهَ الَّذِيْ لَا تَضِيْعُ وَدَائِعُهُ . . .«} $$

> 'I leave you in the keeping of Allah, the One who never fails His trust.'

The Prophet explained this in another hadith:

Certainly, whenever Allah takes charge of something, He protects it.

The important thing is to always remember that whenever you are away from your home, there is One there who never leaves, and He is Allah; and if you want your family to have protection, then put them in the safe keeping of Allah. When you return, you will find them safe. It is a fact that, in most cases travel has the effect of lifting the veil concealing a person's true identity, and of removing the artificial props with which so many people support themselves. For these reasons while a person is on a trip his awareness of what he finds and what he has left behind is significantly heightened.

The *du'as* of the Prophet, upon him be peace, reflect this fact with astonishing subtlety.

Once a man came to him and said: 'I want to set out on a journey. Will you give me provisions?' The Prophet answered,

$$\text{«زَوَّدَكَ اللهُ التَّقْوَى وَغَفَرَ ذَنْبَكَ وَيَسَّرَ لَكَ الْخَيْرَ}$$
$$\text{حَيْثُ كُنْتَ».}$$

'May Allah provide you with a store of *taqwa*.' The man said, 'Give me more.' The Prophet said, 'And may He forgive your sins.' The man said, 'Give me more.' The Prophet said, 'And may He facilitate good for you wherever you may be.'

Abu Hurayrah related that a man said,

'O Rasulullah! I want to go on a journey. Please give me some advice.' The Prophet said, 'Heed Allah, and make *takbir* as you reach the top of every hill.' And as the man turned to go, he went on:

$$\text{«اَللّٰهُمَّ اطْوِلَهُ الْبُعْدَ، وَهَوِّنْ عَلَيْهِ السَّفَرَ».}$$

'O Allah, fold the distances for him, and make his journey easy for him.'

Travel today is not as arduous as it used to be. Roads have been constructed to allow motor vehicles to transport people in comfort. If they wish, they may move over the earth's surface in these wonderful inventions, or far above it in the clouds. Travel times have dwindled so much that what once took months and great exertion now takes a few hours and a little inconvenience. But, despite these available comforts, the dangers to be encountered on land, on sea, and in the air have not vanished, though they have certainly diminished.

While even the slightest danger remains, there is always a possibility that one will fall into it. Stories of disasters befalling people on their travels are common. Thus it is sheer madness for a person to believe himself beyond the need of God's protection. Even today the death toll from highway and other travel related accidents is far greater than the toll exacted by plague and disease.

Death waits in ambush for every man, wherever he may wander to; His time will come and then, he'll find, there's nothing that a man can do.

The *adab* or code of exemplary conduct of the Prophet, upon him be peace, with regard to travel encourages the traveler to actively seek the protection of Allah, and to expect to see the workings of His infinite mercy. Whenever one of his people set out on a journey, 'Abd Allah ibn 'Umar would say to him:

Come close to me so that I may say goodbye to you the way that the Prophet used to say goodbye to us. He used to say:

«أَسْتَوْدِعُ اللَّهَ دِيْنَكَ، وَأَمَانَتَكَ، وَخَوَاتِيْمَ عَمَلِكَ».

'I commit your *din* (religious conviction) to the keeping of Allah, and (so also) your responsibilities, and the outcome of your doings.

71

'Abd Allah said: 'Whenever the Prophet said goodbye to anyone, he would hold his hand. Finally, it would be the one leaving who would disengage his hand from the Prophet's grasp, upon him be peace.'

Here we encounter emotions both stirring and animated. The Prophet holds the traveler's hand until the latter decides to go about his business. It is then that the Prophet asks of Allah three things for the traveler; to protect his *din*, to aid him in living up to his responsibilities, and to ensure that his efforts result in a fruitful outcome. The traveler may make a mistake or even stumble headlong, but he will pull himself up again, straighten himself out, and then go on to complete in the best possible manner, whatever it was he set out to do.

Indeed, what more could a traveler need? Except, perhaps, the continually renewed perception that Allah is blessing him with gift after gift. In another hadith it is related by 'Ali ibn Rabi'ah that:

> I saw 'Ali ibn Abi Talib, may Allah be pleased with him, presented with a horse to ride. When he placed his foot in the stirrup (to mount), he said: *Bismillah*. When he had settled himself in the saddle, he said:

> '*Al hamdu li Allah*, Glory be to the One who has made all this subservient to our use since (but for Him) we would not have been able to attain to it. Hence, it is unto our Lord that we must always turn.'

Then he said *Al hamdu li Allah* three times, and *Allahu Akbar* three times, and then he recited the following:

$$\text{«سُبْحَانَ الَّذِي سَخَّرَ لَنَا هٰذَا وَمَا كُنَّا لَهُ مُقْرِنِينَ وَإِنَّا إِلَىٰ رَبِّنَا لَمُنْقَلِبُونَ».}$$

'Glory to you, O Allah, I have done wrong, so forgive me. Surely no one can forgive me of my wrongdoing except You.'

Then 'Ali ibn Abi Talib laughed. When he was asked what it was that caused him to laugh, he replied:

'Once I saw the Prophet do exactly as I have done just now, and then laugh, so I asked him why he had laughed. He replied,

«سُبْحَانَكَ اللَّهُمَّ إِنِّي ظَلَمْتُ نَفْسِي فَاغْفِرْ لِي، فَإِنَّهُ لَا يَغْفِرُ الذُّنُوبَ إِلَّا أَنْتَ».

"Your Lord is pleased with His servant when, in the knowledge that there is no one else who can forgive him, he asks the Lord to forgive him his wrongdoing."'

When a servant commits a wrong, he does something most unsavory and unbecoming. In relation to Allah, that wrong doing takes on the further aspect of transgression and insolence. He does these thing as a result of being overcome by passion, or by distorted thinking. But for how long will he remain under the influence of his passions, or his warped ideas? Undoubtedly Allah awaits the return of those who stray, and rejoices with the repentance of His servant, and appreciates every step in His direction taken by that servant. It is an excellent thing that a servant acknowledge his mistake, feel the enormity of what he has done, and then return in shame to his Master, the Controller of his destiny.

Some people remain stationary, enveloped in their own mistakes like some defeated army surrounded by an enemy waiting to deliver the final blow! Others come to their senses before it is too late, and hasten to their Lord, saying:

O Lord, we do believe. Then forgive us our sins, and deliver us from the torment of the Fire. (Al 'Imran 3: 16)

In so saying, the forgetful man remembers, the stray returns, and he learns that he has a Lord who seizes and forgives, who punishes and blesses. How did he forget in the first place? What caused him to stray? Now he feels his own weakness and depravity, aware that it is Allah alone who can treat his wounds and restore his health:

> And those who, when they commit an indecency or do wrong to themselves, remember Allah and seek forgiveness for their sins—and who but Allah can forgive one's sins— and do not knowingly persist in what they do. (Al 'Imran 3: 135)

Assuredly, those who turn to God are better guided than those who persist in their wrongdoing, or those who seek forgiveness from people like themselves.

One might ask here why this particular *du'a* should have been pre-scribed for recital at the beginning of a journey?

The reason is that the prospect of a lengthy journey will often create great anxiety in the traveler, especially if he has to leave his family and loved ones behind. His state at that time is one which takes him closer to his Lord and makes him more acutely aware of the wrongs he has done in the past, so that his lips naturally move in quest of mercy and forgiveness.

In another hadith it is related that when the Prophet, upon him be peace, mounted his camel with the intention of setting out on a trip he would say, after beginning with *Allahu Akbar*:

«اَللّٰهُمَّ إِنَّا نَسْأَلُكَ فِي سَفَرِنَا هٰذَا الْبِرَّ وَالتَّقْوٰى، وَمِنَ الْعَمَلِ مَا تَرْضٰى . . . اَللّٰهُمَّ هَوِّنْ عَلَيْنَا سَفَرَنَا هٰذَا، وَاطْوِ عَنَّا بُعْدَهُ، أَنْتَ الصَّاحِبُ فِي السَّفَرِ وَالْخَلِيفَةُ فِي الأَهْلِ ، اَللّٰهُمَّ إِنِّي أَعُوذُ بِكَ مِنْ وَعْثَاءِ السَّفَرِ، وَسُوءِ الْمُنْقَلَبِ، وَكَآبَةِ الْمَنْظَرِ فِي الأَهْلِ وَالْمَالِ . . . .»

74

O Allah, we ask You of this, our journey, righteousness and *taqwa*; and of deeds, those which are pleasing to You. O Allah, make this, our journey, easy for us, and fold its distances (so as to make it shorter for us). You are our Companion in travel and the Protector of those we leave behind. O Allah, I seek refuge in You from the hardship of the journey ahead, and from wandering into evil, and from harm befalling my family or wealth.

On return from the journey, he would repeat the same *du'a* and then, upon him be peace, add the following:

«آيِبُونَ تَائِبُونَ عَابِدُونَ لِرَبِّنَا حَامِدُونَ».

Returning, repenting, worshipping, praising Our Lord.

It is also recorded that the Prophet upon him be peace, and his Companions would say *Allahu Akbar* whenever they journeyed over the crest of a hill, and that they said *Subhan Allah* whenever they reached the valley floor. It was as if the entire caravan was performing salah, saying *Subhan Allah* in *sajdah* on the valley floors and *Allahu Akbar* on every hill.

What a noble life it is that makes its chief occupation the glorification of Allah. And makes *dhikr* and praise of Him the sort of wealth which soothes the aching body and causes time to pass unnoticed! Indeed, Muhammad, peace be upon him, transformed the face of the earth into a heavenly place, filled with angels, and not mere mortals!

I once traveled with a small group of Arab students. When our plane began its descent toward a large Arabian city, I suddenly felt anxious for the future of the young people with me after our landing, thinking to myself: 'Where will they stay, what kind of people will they live with, what manner of human demons lie in wait for their arrival?' Even as I was thus engaged, I heard the voices of a group of them beseeching Allah with the *du'a* recommended for recital on such an occasion. And I said to myself: They will not be lost, be it the will of Allah. Now, of that *du'a* they recited. It is related that the Prophet, upon him be peace, never caught sight of a town he proposed to enter without immediately uttering the following words:

«اَللّٰهُمَّ رَبَّ السَّمٰوَاتِ السَّبْعِ وَمَا أَظْلَلْنَ، وَالْأَرَضِينَ السَّبْعِ وَمَا أَقْلَلْنَ، وَرَبَّ الشَّيَاطِينِ وَمَا أَضْلَلْنَ، وَرَبَّ الرِّيَاحِ وَمَا أَذْرَيْنَ، أَسْأَلُكَ خَيْرَ هٰذِهِ الْقَرْيَةِ، وَخَيْرَ أَهْلِهَا، وَخَيْرَ مَا فِيهَا، وَأَعُوذُ بِكَ مِنْ شَرِّهَا، وَشَرِّ أَهْلِهَا، وَشَرِّ مَا فِيهَا....»

O Allah, Lord of the Seven Heavens and all that they shadow, Lord of the Seven Earths and all that they conceal, Lord of the Satans and all that they lead astray, Lord of the winds and all that they carry, I ask you for the good of this village, the good of its people, and whatever good is within it, as I seek refuge in You from the evil of the village, the evil of its people, and whatever evil is within it.

In another hadith it is recorded that, whenever he approached a village he intended to enter, he would say, upon him be peace:

«اَللّٰهُمَّ إِنِّي أَسْأَلُكَ مِنْ خَيْرِ هٰذِهِ، وَخَيْرِ مَا جَمَعْتَ فِيهَا، وَأَعُوذُ بِكَ مِنْ شَرِّهَا، وَشَرِّ مَا جَمَعْتَ فِيهَا، اَللّٰهُمَّ ارْزُقْنِي حَبَاهَا، وَأَعِذْنَا مِنْ وَبَاهَا، وَحَبِّبْنَا إِلٰى أَهْلِهَا، وَحَبِّبْ صَالِحِيْ أَهْلِهَا إِلَيْنَا....»

O Allah, I ask You for the good of this (place) and the good You have gathered within it. I seek refuge in You from the evil of it, and the evil You have gathered in it. O Allah!

Sustain us through those who live here, and protect us from disease in this place, and make the inhabitants to love us as you make us to love the righteous ones among them.

These supplications encompass all the desires of a traveler newly arrived in an unknown place; they animate him in the knowledge that his ultimate return is unto Allah, that his affairs are in His hands, and that he can rest assured that, regardless of the direction in which he may be traveling, the Almighty will suffice him.

Even when breaking a journey, the Prophet, upon him be peace, never once diverted his attention from seeking the company and protection of Allah. Total dependence on Allah is an essential characteristic of every believer, and one which frees him from dependence on other humans, and which shields him from their troubles. Khawlah bint al Hakim related that she heard the Prophet, upon him be peace, say:

Whoever breaks a journey and says:

$$\text{«أَعُوذُ بِكَلِمَاتِ اللّٰهِ التَّامَّاتِ مِنْ شَرِّ مَا خَلَقَ».}$$

'I seek refuge in the comprehensive promises of Allah from the evil of what He created,' will come to no harm for as long as he remains at that stopping place.

The 'comprehensive promises' of Allah are the means by which He perfects His bounty on His creation from the treasure troves of His mercy so that they never have need of any other. Consider the following verses of the Qur'an:

And thus your Sustainer's good promise to the children of Israel was fulfilled as a result of their patience in adversity. (al A'raf 7: 137)

For, truly and justly has your Sustainer's promise been ful-filled. There is no power that could alter (the fulfillment of) His promises. (al An'am 6: 116)

Of course, the promises referred to here are formal rather than bind-ing in any way, so that in fact Allah fulfills them out of His benevo-lence for those who supplicate and seek Him.

Abdullah ibn 'Umar related that whenever the Prophet, upon him be peace, set out on a journey at night, he would first say:

$$\text{«يَاأَرْضُ، رَبِّي وَرَبُّكِ اللَّهُ، أَعُوذُ بِاللَّهِ مِنْ شَرِّكِ وَشَرِّ مَا فِيكِ، وَشَرِّ مَا خُلِقَ فِيكِ، وَشَرِّ مَا يَدِبُّ عَلَيْكِ».}$$

O Earth! Your Lord and my Lord is Allah. So I seek refuge in Allah from your evil, from the evil within you, from the evil created within you, and from the evil of what creeps over you.

$$\text{«أَعُوذُ بِكَ مِنْ أَسَدٍ وَأَسْوَدَ، وَمِنَ الْحَيَّةِ وَالْعَقْرَبِ، وَمِنْ شَرِّ سَاكِنِ الْبَلَدِ، وَمِنْ وَالِدٍ، وَمَا وَلَدَ».}$$

I seek refuge in Allah from lion and evil eyes, from snake and scorpion, from the evil of the city dweller, and from the begetter and what he begets.

As to the meaning of 'the begetter and what he begets', it has been said that it is Iblis and his offspring who are intended:

Will you then take him (Iblis) and his offspring for (your) masters instead of Me, although they are your foes? (al Kahf 18: 50)

Empty terrain, especially the desert, abounds in flying and creeping vermin, so that the traveler naturally seeks protection from the things which lie hidden within it, and which flit across its surface. When at last the traveler returns to his home and loved ones, it is only fitting that he should give thanks to his Lord by saying:

«الْحَمْدُ لِلَّهِ الَّذِيْ بِنِعْمَتِهِ تَتِمُّ الصَّالِحَاتُ».

All praise to Allah by whose blessings all good things are brought to fulfillment!

Indeed, these are words which should be said on every happy occasion. And the traveler's family should reply with the following words:

«الْحَمْدُ لِلَّهِ الَّذِيْ جَمَعَ الشَّمْلَ بِكَ».

All praise to Allah who has gathered through you what was scattered.

or

«الْحَمْدُ لِلَّهِ الَّذِيْ سَلَّمَكَ».

All praise to Allah who has (brought you back) safely.

It is related that when the Prophet, upon him be peace, returned from one of his military campaigns, he was greeted by his wife, 'A'ishah, who took his hand and said:

All praise to Allah who has led you to victory, caused you to be respected, and treated you with honor!

The people of his time perceived that the Prophet of Allah, upon him be peace, was the most devoted of all God's creatures, the most hopeful of His mercy, and the most constant in His remembrance and praise. It should come as little surprise, then, that those people used to go to him, whenever they were beset with difficulties, in order to seek his *du'a* (to Allah on their behalf) and to anticipate with him the descent of divine blessings.

It is related by 'A'ishah that people complained to the Prophet, upon him be peace, of drought. He ordered that a *minbar* be erected outside in the place reserved for prayer on festival days and that all should meet there on an appointed day. On that day the Prophet, upon him be peace, came out shortly after sunrise and sat on the *minbar*. After beginning with *Allahu Akbar* and *al hamdu li Allah*, he said:

> You have complained of drought in the land, and the failure of the rains to arrive in their usual time. Allah has commanded you to supplicate Him, and He has promised that (if you do so) He will answer you.

Thereafter he said:

$$ \text{,الْحَمْدُ لِلَّهِ رَبِّ الْعَالَمِينَ الرَّحْمٰنِ الرَّحِيمِ مَالِكِ يَوْمِ الدِّينِ، لَا إِلٰهَ إِلَّا اللَّهُ يَفْعَلُ مَا يُرِيدُ. اللَّهُمَّ أَنْتَ اللَّهُ لَا إِلٰهَ إِلَّا أَنْتَ، أَنْتَ الْغَنِيُّ وَنَحْنُ الْفُقَرَاءُ، أَنْزِلْ عَلَيْنَا الْغَيْثَ، وَاجْعَلْ مَا أَنْزَلْتَ لَنَا قُوَّةً وَبَلَاغاً إِلَى حِينٍ،. } $$

> Praise to Allah! Lord of the Worlds, Merciful and Mercy Giving, Master of the Day of Reckoning! There is no God but Allah, He does as He wills. O Allah! You are Allah, and there is no God but You. You are the Self Sufficient and we are the needful! Send the rains down upon us, and make of what You send down to us our strength and sustenance for a time.

Then he lifted his hands so high that one could see the white of his armpits, turned his back to the people, tossed his cloak from one shoulder to the other, and then again faced the people. After that he stood and prayed two *rak'ahs* of salah.

Then Allah, Exalted is He, caused clouds to form in the sky, and lightning and thunder, after which it rained by His will. The Prophet, upon him be peace, had not yet reached his mosque when the rains became a flood. He said:

> I give witness that Allah is Powerful over everything, and that I am Allah's servant and Prophet.

A foolish youth once asked me if I could give rational proof of the existence of Allah. I answered him as kindly as I could, saying: 'I know Him through direct experience.' He said, 'What do you mean by direct experience?' I said, 'A wandering orphan knows by reason that he has a father, even though he may never have seen him. But a son who lives with his father has no need for such reasoning since he has the constant love and affection of his father day in and day out. Such a one knows his father through direct experience, like I have explained to you.'

During my lifetime I have asked Allah for things which only He could have brought about. And He, may He be praised, has always answered my requests. So how can I not know Him after all of that? An Arab poet once wrote to the effect that a favor shown to a snarling dog will work wonders. What, then, of a favor done for an intelligent human being?

Let us return to the Sahabah when drought confronted them and heat threatened to destroy their crops and livestock. They went to the Prophet so that he could petition the Lord. He had barely finished leading them in prayer before the skies began to overflow and give tidings of a gleaming springtime. After this, and all that they had witnessed, can you imagine what kind of faith they must have had? Surely they had gone beyond the stage of faith based on reason to a purer and more advanced stage. All that the Prophet, upon him be peace, said after the rain began to pour down was:

> I give witness that Allah is Powerful over everything, and that I am Allah's servant and Prophet.

Obviously, witnessing (*shahadah*), under such circumstances, is a stage far beyond merely nominal faith.

The naive youth then said to me: 'We have learned in school that matter is eternal, constant, the particles of which are both indestructible and incapable of being reproduced. This is something which has rocked my faith to such an extent that had I not felt the conviction in your words, I would never again have been a believer.'

'Young man', I said, 'the people who formulated that theory have propounded a half truth after giving a distorted version of the facts. The truth of the matter is that the Lord of all matter is eternal; He has neither been created nor will He ever be destroyed. You and I, on the other hand, came into existence after being nothing. You and I are anything but eternal. Can you tell me who created us in our mothers' wombs? Can you tell me what it was that pushed us out into the world when our bodies had formed completely after being fetuses and, before that, merely groupings of cells?'

I do not care for unreasonableness in argument; may I be spared the ridiculing of the materialists. A child might suppose that movement in a mirror image comes directly from the image itself, or from the polished surface of the glass. But, certainly, it will not be long before the same child realizes that the movement he sees comes from the body reflected in the mirror, and not from the reflection itself! Yet, countless people in their intellectual childhood ascribe to dull matter things of which it is utterly incapable. I ask such people: 'Who fashioned the infinite variety of fingerprint designs so that no two are ever alike? Or, for that matter, who created skin? These things are brought into existence and are not, on their own, capable of bringing themselves (or anything else) into existence.'

But let us forget about the world of the body, and all that is within it of seemingly miraculous order, for an even more sublime world. Who created intelligence? Or the rashness or patience in our personalities? Should we look around for some kind of 'Unknown Soldier' who is responsible for all this? Or a chemical formula?

Unreasoning people deliberately turn themselves away from Allah and attempt to ignore His supreme power with simple minded impudence. But that is not what is so amazing. The amazing thing is that those same people insist on describing themselves as 'educated', 'modern' and other such epithets.

The fact is that people from the earliest times to the present have denied the works of Allah in His creation and, instead, have ascribed those works to the nearest available cause/manifestation, like a child ascribing the motion of a reflection in a mirror to the reflection itself.

Zayn ibn Khalid al Juhani related that once, at Hudaybiyah, as the Prophet of Allah, upon him be peace, led the Muslims in morning prayer after a light rain, he turned to those assembled and said:

'Do you know what your Lord says?' The Muslims replied: 'Allah and His Prophet know best.' He said: 'Allah says, "Some of My servants have risen as believers in Me, while others have risen as *kafir*. As to those who said that the rain has fallen by the bounty and mercy of Allah, those are the believers in Me. But as to those who said that the rain came due to a certain alignment in the heavens, those are the *kafirs*, believers in the stars."'

Without a doubt, those who suppose that things come into existence without divine decree or supervision — and such people today are clearly in the majority — are truly disbelievers. As for those who know that Allah is the Creator of all things, the Giver of all Good, they are truly believers. And they are believers regardless of whether they ascribe His works to Him directly or to a secondary cause from among His creation, figuratively. For example, one who says that the summer ripened the fruit, meaning that the summer sun was a secondary cause for the ripening of the fruit, is a believer. His words are not blasphemous because he says them in the knowledge that Allah is the One who causes seeds to germinate and then, of His bounty, brings the plants to fruition.

The fault is with the one whose heart and mind are so barren that they contain nothing of the remembrance of Allah; those who ascribe things and events to the most obvious of causes and refuse to acknowledge the role of the Almighty behind all that occurs. Indeed, from time to time the Prophet, upon him be peace, used to lift the veil from over the normal causes of certain phenomena so as to explain their true value and thereby bring people closer to their Lord, and to remembrance of Him.

Allah, in His kindness, sometimes deprives His servants of the things they need so that they turn to Him in supplication, and implore Him to help them. Then when He gives them what they want, their hearts are watered from the well of true thanksgiving. It is in this way that they gain an increase in their faith.

The different prayers of *istisqa'* (seeking rain), *istikharah* (seeking guidance) and *hajah* (need) were all prescribed for this very reason.

I myself have seen how the people of Makkah hasten to prayer (*istisqa'*) whenever the rains are late in coming, so that within a matter of days the rains come tumbling down.

And we recorded earlier how quickly Allah answered the prayer of the Prophet, upon him be peace, so that he was nearly carried away in a flood after having, only minutes before, prayed for rain to be sent to the dry and parched land around Madinah.

Is it not strange that while the eastern part of Africa, and parts of the West, should be continually caught in the grip of drought and famine, the idea of prayer (*istisqa'*) has yet to occur to anyone, as if Allah is neither known nor sought? These are clearly the signs of a materialist civilization and its influence as carried by the colonialist powers to the lands they victimized.

11

WORLDLY TRAVAILS

Very often it happens that a man is so weakened by his troubles that he becomes pitiful; or so strengthened by his successes that he becomes tyrannical. But the intelligent believer should not go astray, nor should he exceed the proper bounds; he should persevere in his practice of Islam in both adversity and prosperity.

No man, as long as he remains alive, will ever be wholly free of trial. This is simply the nature of things in this world. Suffering uncovers human frailties and literally pushes the reasonable person to his knees, so to speak, at Allah's door, in quest of relief and the mercy of his Lord. The true believer is expected to seek refuge in Allah in every trouble which befalls him, regardless of how insignificant it may seem. The Prophet of Allah, upon him be peace, said:

> Let each of you turn unto Allah in every troublesome matter; even when you are pained by the thong of your sandal, for even that is a trial.

In other words, the Muslim must rely, in all of his affairs, upon Allah's assistance, and not suppose that any of these affairs can be settled except by His leave. The greater the misfortune, the more ardent the Muslim's desire for refuge in Allah, and the more protracted his entreaty. Thauban related that the Prophet, upon him be peace, whenever he encountered anything awesome, would say:

> He is Allah. Allah is my Lord. He has no partner.

The Prophet taught his Companions, whenever they felt the presence of fear, to say:

«أَعُوذُ بِكَلِمَاتِ اللّهِ التَّامَّةِ مِنْ غَضَبِهِ، وَشَرِّ عِبَادِهِ،
وَمِنْ هَمَزَاتِ الشَّيَاطِينِ وَأَنْ يَحْضُرُونِ».

I seek refuge through Allah's perfect words from His wrath, from the evil of His servants, and from the whispering of satanic forces and from their presence.

Zayd ibn Thabit related that when he complained to the Prophet, upon him be peace, of insomnia, he urged him to repeat this *du'a:*

«اللّهُمَّ غَارَتِ النُّجُومُ، وَهَدَأَتِ الْعُيُونُ، وَأَنْتَ حَيٌّ
قَيُّومٌ لَا تَأْخُذُكَ سِنَةٌ وَلَا نَوْمٌ. .يَاحَيُّ يَاقَيُّومُ أَهْدِيءْ
لَيْلِي وَأَنِمْ عَيْنِي».

O Lord! the stars are out, the eyes are at rest, and You are the Living, the Everlasting who is never taken by drowsiness or sleep. O Living! O Everlasting! Put peace into my night, and sleep into my eyes.

Zayd related that, after he had recited this *du'a* that same evening, Allah relieved him of the burden He had set upon him.

It would seem that the Prophet, upon him be peace, has here interpreted the *Ayat al Kursi*, or at least the first few words of it, in such a way as to help the man in need of sleep to address the Heavenly Monarch who directs all that occurs in the day and the night, and yet is never wearied, never negligent. When a person stands, in the frame of his own weakness, before the possessor of Majesty and Sovereignty, he cannot but come away with a full share of goodness.

We are commanded to call Allah by His beautiful names, and He loves to be praised. For this reason the Prophet, upon him be peace, taught us to persist and implore, by saying, "O Possessor of Majesty and Honor."'

We have said earlier that the Prophet, upon him be peace, was the most learned of all mankind in the ways of Allah, the most heedful of Him, the best endowed with insight into the domains of Allah's beautiful names, and the quickest to perceive what those names demand in the way of patience, thanksgiving, greetings and praise. It has become apparent to all historians and biographers of the Prophet, upon him be peace, that his experiences, both before and after receiving his prophetic mission, contributed to produce in his person such a level of human perfection as had never before been attained on earth. But, of course, no one in creation, no matter what his powers, may impose his friendship on the Almighty. Rather, it is the Creator Allah who, if it be His wish, appoints friends from among His creatures. After making His choice, the Almighty brings about events which heighten the creature's appreciation and so increase his reward. Usually, these events come in the form of major calamities which banish both ease and stability.

Thus, the Last of the Prophets, upon him be peace, began his life as an orphan in need of someone to care for him and cherish him. But Allah took him in. He began his life as a stray, unable to find his way and knowing nothing of the meaning of life. But Allah taught and guided him. Indeed, he was a poor man toiling to make a living and traveling throughout the land in order to maintain himself and his honor. But Allah sufficed him. To confirm this, Allah, Exalted is He, revealed these verses:

> Has He not found you an orphan and given you shelter? And found you lost on your way, and guided you? And found you in want, and given you sufficiency? Therefore, the orphan, never wrong him. And he who seeks your help, never repulse. And of your Lord's blessing, ever speak. (al Duha 93: 6-11)

The middle one, that of guidance after straying, required an entire Qur'anic chapter for its proper explanation. This is the chapter entitled *al Inshirah*, or *al Sharh*. For, indeed, the Prophet of Islam, upon him be peace, grew up in an atmosphere clouded by the backward practices of the pagan Arabs. Though even that was preferable to an atmosphere polluted with deception and falsehood such as that maintained by the Christians and Jews of those times.

The Prophet loathed pagan ways, just as he refused to accept the distortions of the Christians and Jews. Then, what was he to do? Nothing? Through the purity of his nature he gravitated toward isolation, anguished at his own situation and the state of those around him. Unable to enlighten others or himself, where could he turn?

A person of fine sensibilities is inevitably distressed by personal or intellectual problems. Indeed, life for such a person would appear more constricting than even the eye of a needle. The world's riches, if offered to him, would be of no consolation at all. This is how Muhammad lived until revelation came upon him unexpectedly.

In reference to his state at that time, the Almighty said:

Have We not opened up your heart? (al Sharh 94: 1)

That is, by inspiring you with spiritual truths.

And lifted from you the burden that had weighed so heavily on your back. (al Sharh 94: 2-3)

The burden was such that you were forced to flee the society of others, and grieve for yourself and for them, alone and bewildered, and suffer through your incapacity and your exile from your native surroundings.

Then Allah chose you; and who could be more exalted than one chosen by the Lord of the heavens and earth to be His instrument of guidance for all the world?

And have We not raised you high in dignity? (al Sharh 94: 4)

And so is human life:

And, behold, with every hardship comes ease: and, verily, with every hardship comes ease. (al Sharh 94: 5-6)

Finally, what is sought of you, after you have finished your work, is to begin it afresh:

Hence, when you are freed (from distress), remain steadfast, and unto your Lord turn with love. (Sharh 94: 7-8)

And thus we witness accommodation after estrangement, guidance after confusion and hesitation, sufficiency after want. Without a doubt the deprivations suffered by the Prophet, upon him be peace, in his own lifetime made him all the more sensitive to the troubles of others. Thus, he shared their grief, and always did his best to eliminate, or at least to lessen, the troubling factor, regardless of whether the trouble was material or spiritual in nature. His desire was to free his life of it, and the lives of others.

And whose countenance and succor are sought in times of hardship and tribulation? Allah, and none other! Surely, He is the Secure Refuge, the Fortified Sanctuary!

The Prophet, upon him be peace, regularly remembered his Lord, and supplicated Him earnestly and with civility. And, when he took the name of the Lord in fervent prayer, he was urging the multitude: this is the way, so follow it; this is the goal, so seek after it.

And if My servants ask you about Me behold, I am near; I respond to the call of him who calls, whenever he calls unto Me: let them, then, respond unto Me, and believe in Me, so that they might follow the right way. (al Baqarah 2: 186)

Certainly, Muhammad, upon him be peace, was not a priest who would say to the sinners: 'Come to me in confession, and I will forgive you', or 'come to me burdened and oppressed, and I will set you free.' On the contrary, he would say:

> Pray to Allah with me. Pray to Allah for yourselves. You and I, and everyone in the heavens are nothing but that Allah wills to make something out of us. It is He who grants aid and is never aided, and He who orders and never has His orders reversed.

> And if Allah should touch you with misfortune, there is none who can remove it but He; and if He should touch you with good fortune, it is He who has the power to will anything. (al An'am 6: 17)

In this connection, I shall list some of the *du'a* the Prophet used, upon him be peace, to supplicate his Lord, and urged his followers to do the same:

«اَللّٰهُمَّ إِنِّي أَسْأَلُكَ مُوجِبَاتِ رَحْمَتِكَ، وَعَزَائِمَ مَغْفِرَتِكَ، وَالسَّلاَمَةَ مِنْ كُلِّ إِثْمٍ، وَالغَنِيْمَةَ مِنْ كُلِّ بِرٍّ، وَالفَوْزَ بِالْجَنَّةِ، وَالنَّجَاةَ مِنَ النَّارِ».

O Allah! I seek of You that which will make certain (for me) Your mercy, and the resolution of Your forgiveness, as well as freedom from every offense and a share in every virtue, and entry to Paradise, and freedom from the Fire.

«اَللّٰهُمَّ أَلْهِمْنِيْ رُشْدِيْ، وَأَعِذْنِي مِنْ شَرِّ نَفْسِيْ».

O Allah! Inspire me with guidance, and spare me the evil of my selfishness.

90

«اَللّٰهُمَّ إِنِّيْ أَعُوْذُ بِكَ مِنَ الْجُوْعِ فَإِنَّهُ بِئْسَ الضَّجِيْعُ، وَأَعُوْذُ بِكَ مِنَ الْخِيَانَةِ فَإِنَّهَا بِئْسَتِ الْبِطَانَةُ».

O Allah! I seek refuge in You from hunger; for it is a terrible bedfellow. And I seek refuge in You from treachery; for it is indeed a foul inner lining.

«اَللّٰهُمَّ إِنِّيْ أَعُوْذُ بِكَ مِنَ الْبَرَصِ، وَالْجُنُوْنِ، وَالْجُذَامِ، وَسَيِّءِ الْأَسْقَامِ».

O Allah! I seek refuge in You from leprosy, madness, and all horrible illness.

«اَللّٰهُمَّ إِنِّيْ أَعُوْذُ بِكَ مِنْ شَرِّ سَمْعِيْ، وَمِنْ شَرِّ بَصَرِيْ، وَمِنْ شَرِّ لِسَانِيْ وَمِنْ شَرِّ قَلْبِيْ».

O Allah! I seek refuge in You from the evil of my hearing, the evil of my sight, the evil of my tongue, and the evil of my heart.

«اَللّٰهُمَّ إِنِّيْ أَعُوْذُ بِكَ مِنْ فِتْنَةِ النَّارِ، وَعَذَابِ النَّارِ وَمِنْ شَرِّ الْغِنَى وَالْفَقْرِ».

O Allah! I seek refuge in You from the trial of the Fire, and the torment of the Fire, and from the evils of poverty and of wealth.

«اَللّٰهُمَّ إِنِّيْ أَعُوْذُ بِكَ مِنْ مُنْكَرَاتِ الْأَخْلَاقِ، وَالْأَعْمَالِ، وَالْأَهْوَاءِ».

O Allah I seek refuge in You from reprehensible morals, actions and desires.

«اَللّٰهُمَّ إِنِّيْ أَعُوْذُ بِكَ مِنَ العَجْزِ وَالْكَسَلِ وَالْبُخْلِ
وَالْهَرَمِ وَعَذَابِ القَبْرِ».

O Allah! 1 seek refuge in You from incapacity and sloth, from miserliness and decrepitude, and from the torment of the grave.

«اَللّٰهُمَّ آتِ نَفْسِي تَقْوَاهَا وَزَكِّهَا أَنْتَ خَيْرُ مَنْ زَكَّاهَا
أَنْتَ وَلِيُّهَا وَمَوْلَاهَا».

O Allah! Grant my soul consciousness of You and purify it. You are the Best to purify. You are the soul's Compassion and its Master.

«اَللّٰهُمَّ إِنِّيْ أَعُوْذُ بِكَ مِنْ عِلْمٍ لَا يَنْفَعُ، وَمِنْ قَلْبٍ
لَا يَخْشَعُ، وَمِنْ نَفْسٍ لَا تَشْبَعُ، وَمِنْ دَعْوَةٍ لَا
يُسْتَجَابُ لَهَا».

O Allah! I seek refuge in You from knowledge which does not benefit, from a heart which is not humble, from an inner self which is never satisfied, and from a prayer which is not answered.

«اَللّٰهُمَّ إِنِّيْ أَعُوْذُ بِكَ مِنْ زَوَالِ نِعْمَتِكَ، وَتَحَوُّلِ
عَافِيَتِكَ، وَفُجَاءَةِ نِقْمَتِكَ، وَجَمِيعِ سَخَطِكَ».

O Allah! I seek refuge in You from the withdrawal of Your favor, the decline of the good health you have given, the suddenness of Your vengeance, and from all forms of Your wrath.

«اَللّٰهُمَّ إِنِّيْ أَعُوْذُ بِكَ مِنْ شَرِّ مَا عَمِلْتُ، وَمِنْ شَرِّ مَا لَمْ أَعْمَلْ».

O Allah! I seek refuge in You from the evil of what I have done, and the evil of what I have not done.

«اِغْفِرْ لِيْ خَطِيْئَتِيْ وَجَهْلِيْ، وَإِسْرَافِيْ فِيْ أَمْرِيْ، وَمَا أَنْتَ أَعْلَمُ بِهِ مِنِّيْ».

Forgive me my wrongs and my ignorance, my excesses I with myself, and all that You know better than I.

«اِغْفِرْ لِيْ جِدِّيْ وَهَزْلِيْ، وَخَطَئِيْ وَعَمَدِيْ، وَكُلُّ ذَلِكَ عِنْدِيْ».

Forgive me (all the wrongs I have committed) in jest and in earnest, intentionally and inadvertently; and all of this is from me.

«اَللّٰهُمَّ إِنِّيْ ظَلَمْتُ نَفْسِيْ ظُلْمًا كَثِيْرًا، وَلَا يَغْفِرُ الذُّنُوْبَ إِلَّا أَنْتَ، فَاغْفِرْ لِيْ مَغْفِرَةً مِنْ عِنْدِكَ، وَارْحَمْنِيْ إِنَّكَ أَنْتَ الْغَفُوْرُ الرَّحِيْمُ».

O Allah! Verily I have wronged my soul greatly. And no one can forgive sins but You. So forgive me with Your forgiveness, and have mercy upon me. You are the Merciful, Forgiving.

«اللّٰهُمَّ اهْدِنِيْ وَسَدِّدْنِيْ».

O Allah! Guide me, and put me aright.

«اَللّٰهُمَّ إِنِّيْ أَعُوْذُ بِكَ مِنَ الْعَجْزِ وَالْكَسَلِ وَالْجُبْنِ وَالْبُخْلِ وَالْهَرَمِ . وَأَعُوْذُ بِكَ مِنْ عَذَابِ الْقَبْرِ، وَأَعُوْذُ بِكَ مِنْ فِتْنَةِ الْمَحْيَا وَالْمَمَاتِ، وَضَلَعِ الدَّيْنِ، وَغَلَبَةِ الرِّجَالِ» .

O Allah! I seek refuge in You from incapacity, sloth, cowardice, miserliness and decrepitude. And I seek refuge in You from the torment of the grave. And I seek refuge in You from the trials of life and death, the burden of debt and the domination of men.

«اَللّٰهُمَّ اغْفِرْ لِيْ، وَارْحَمْنِيْ، وَعَافِنِيْ، وَارْزُقْنِيْ» .

O Allah! Forgive me, have mercy on me, grant me well being, and sustain me.

«اَللّٰهُمَّ مُصَرِّفَ الْقُلُوْبِ صَرِّفْ قُلُوْبَنَا عَلَىٰ طَاعَتِكَ» .

O Allah! Changer of Hearts! Change our hearts to be obedient to You.

«اَللّٰهُمَّ إِنَّا نَعُوْذُ بِكَ مِنْ جَهْدِ الْبَلَاءِ، وَدَرْكِ الشَّقَاءِ، وَسُوْءِ الْقَضَاءِ، وَشَمَاتَةِ الْأَعْدَاءِ» .

O Allah! We seek refuge in You from the pains of affliction, the depths of misery, the misfortunes of fate, and the malice of enemies.

«اَللّٰهُمَّ اغْفِرْ لِيْ، وَارْحَمْنِيْ، وَاهْدِنِيْ، وَعَافِنِيْ، وَارْزُقْنِيْ»

O Allah! Forgive me, and have mercy on me, and guide me, and grant me well being, and sustain me.

«اَللَّهُمَّ إِنِّي أَسْأَلُكَ الْهُدَى، وَالتُّقَى، وَالْعَفَافَ، وَالْغِنَى».

O Allah! Verily I ask of You guidance, heedfulness, chastity and self sufficiency.

«اَللَّهُمَّ اغْفِرْ لِي ذَنْبِي كُلَّهُ، دِقَّهُ وَجِلَّهُ، وَأَوَّلَهُ وَآخِرَهُ، وَعَلَانِيَتَهُ وَسِرَّهُ».

O Allah! Forgive me my sins totally, the major ones and the minor, the old ones and the new, the manifest ones and the inner.

«اَللَّهُمَّ إِنِّي أَعُوذُ بِكَ مِنْ شَرِّ الْخَلْقِ، وَهَمِّ الرِّزْقِ، وَسُوءِ الْخُلُقِ».

O Allah! I seek refuge in You from the evil of creation, concern over sustenance, and immorality.

«اَللَّهُمَّ إِنِّي أَعُوذُ بِكَ مِنَ الشِّقَاقِ، وَالنِّفَاقِ، وَسُوءِ الْأَخْلَاقِ».

O Allah! I seek refuge in You from controversy, hypocrisy and immorality.

«اَللَّهُمَّ لَكَ الْحَمْدُ كُلُّهُ، وَلَكَ الْمُلْكُ كُلُّهُ، وَبِيَدِكَ الْخَيْرُ كُلُّهُ، عَلَانِيَتُهُ وَسِرُّهُ، وَلَكَ الْحَمْدُ إِنَّكَ عَلَى كُلِّ شَيْءٍ قَدِيرٌ. اغْفِرْ لِي مَا مَضَى مِنْ ذُنُوبِي، وَاعْصِمْنِي فِيمَا بَقِيَ مِنْ عُمُرِي، وَارْزُقْنِي أَعْمَالاً زَاكِيَةً تَرْضَى بِهَا عَنِّي، وَتُبْ عَلَيَّ».

O Allah! All praise is due to You. Yours is all sovereignty. All good is in Your hands, both the hidden good and the manifest. All praise to You, You are powerful over everything. Forgive me those of my sins which have already occurred, and safeguard me (from sin) for what remains of my lifetime, and sustain me with pure deeds which will earn me Your pleasure, and make me penitent.

«اللَّهُمَّ إِنِّي أَعُوذُ بِكَ مِنَ الْفَقْرِ إِلاَّ إِلَيْكَ، وَمِنَ الذُّلِّ إِلاَّ لَكَ، وَمِنَ الْخَوْفِ إِلاَّ مِنْكَ، وَأَعُوذُ بِكَ أَنْ أَقُولَ زُوراً، أَوْ أَغْشَى فُجُوراً، أَوْ أَكُونَ بِكَ مَغْرُوراً، وَأَعُوذُ بِكَ مِنْ شَمَاتَةِ الْأَعْدَاءِ، وَعُضَالِ الدَّاءِ، وَخَيْبَةِ الرَّجَاءِ، وَزَوَالِ النِّعْمَةِ، وَفُجَاءَةِ النِّقْمَةِ».

Allah! I seek refuge in You from need except of You, and from meekness except before You, and from fear except of You. I seek refuge in You from my ever telling an untruth, or perpetrating indecency, or becoming overweening because of (my relationship with) You. I seek refuge in You from the malice of enemies, incurable disease, shattered hope, withdrawal of favor, and the sudden fall of vengeance.

«اَللَّهُمَّ إِنِّي أَعُوذُ بِكَ مِنَ الْعَطَبِ، وَالنَّصَبِ، وَأَعُوذُ بِكَ مِنْ وَعْثَاءِ السَّفَرِ وَسُوْءِ الْمُنْقَلَبِ».

O Allah! I seek refuge in You from ruin and ordeal, and I seek refuge in You from the hardships of traveling and from a final destiny of evil.

«اللَّهُمَّ إِنِّي أَعُوذُ بِكَ مِنَ الزَّيْغِ، وَالْجَزَعِ، وَأَعُوذُ بِكَ مِنَ الطَّمَعِ فِي غَيْرِ مَطْمَعٍ».

O Allah! I seek refuge in You from perversity and anxiety, and I seek refuge in You from aspiring after that which is beyond aspiration.

«اَللّٰهُمَّ إِنِّي أَعُوذُ بِكَ مِنَ الْفِتَنِ مَا ظَهَرَ مِنْهَا وَمَا بَطَنَ، وَأَعُوذُ بِكَلِمَاتِ اللّٰهِ التَّامَّاتِ مِنْ شَرِّ مَا خَلَقَ».

Allah! I seek refuge in You from all trials, those which are public and those which are secret. And I seek refuge in the complete word of Allah from the evil which He created.

«اَللّٰهُمَّ إِنِّي أَعُوذُ بِكَ مِنْ أَنْ أَظْلِمَ أَوْ أُظْلَمَ، أَوْ أَبْغِيَ أَوْ يُبْغَىٰ عَلَيَّ أَوْ أَطْغَىٰ أَوْ يُطْغَىٰ عَلَيَّ».

O Allah! I seek refuge in You from doing wrong and being wronged, from envying and being envied, and from tyrannizing and being tyrannized.

«اَللّٰهُمَّ اجْعَلْنِيْ لَكَ ذَكَّاراً لَكَ شَكَّاراً لَكَ مِطْوَاعاً لَكَ مُخْبِتاً إِلَيْكَ أَوَّاهاً مُنِيْباً. رَبِّ تَقَبَّلْ تَوْبَتِيْ، وَاغْسِلْ حَوْبَتِيْ، وَأَجِبْ دَعْوَتِي، وَثَبِّتْ حُجَّتِيْ، وَاهْدِ قَلْبِي، وَسَدِّدْ لِسَانِي، وَاسْلُلْ سَخِيْمَةَ صَدْرِيْ».

O Allah! Make me oft remembering You, grateful to You, obedient to You, humble before You, sighing, repentant. My Lord, accept my repentance, cleanse (me of) my misdeeds, answer my prayer, substantiate my plea, guide my heart, straighten my tongue and banish all ill will from my breast.

وَاللَّهُمَّ زِدْنَا وَلَا تَنْقُصْنَا، وَأَكْرِمْنَا وَلَا تُهِنَّا، وَآثِرْنَا
وَلَا تُؤْثِرْ عَلَيْنَا، وَأَرْضِنَا وَارْضَ عَنَّا.

O Allah! Grant us increase and do not deprive us. Grant us honor and do not abase us. Grant us preference and do not prefer (others) over us. Grant us Your pleasure and do not be displeased with us.

This much should suffice as a measure of the attention with which Muhammad turned to his Lord. But, before we go on to consider some of what has been reproduced above, let me pose the following question: Was there ever a man in the history of the five continents who loved the Almighty with a greater degree of emotion? Was there ever a man in history who humbled himself before Allah with words more sincere than these?

We Muslims have only this to say to those who find it strange that we follow Muhammad: Show us someone to compare with him, someone who had a purer relationship with Allah, and we will follow him!

It is we, rather, who mourn those who do not recognize Muhammad and, out of ignorance, oppose him. What we find strange is the blindness which prevents them from seeing him (as he truly was).

The hearts of men, when they find guidance in the heart of Muhammad, pulsing, as it were, with the Unity and glorification of Allah; and their limbs, when they submit to his being as they follow him in the postures of prayer (which he taught them to perform) assume, at such moments, their most pure and noble states. Yes, indeed, mature humanity found its finest expression in this eminent individual who had given himself over wholeheartedly to the remembrance of Allah, and to obedience to Him.

Should we assume that everything which possesses a man's heart other than his Lord is an idol, regardless of whether it be wealth, or desire, or love of self, or love of another, then the person who most thoroughly smashed every last idol, and showed man how best to dedicate his life to Allah and no other, was Muhammad, upon whom be the peace and blessings of Allah.

From these *du'as* a number of important attitudes stand out. The first of these is that the Prophet, upon him be peace, hated illness, and incurable disease in particular. Who among us enjoys a fever, or cancer? The desire for good health is both natural and human. Only a pervert enjoys pain. Quite rightly then, the Prophet, upon him be peace, asks his Lord for the well being of his senses and organs, seeking refuge in Him from illness, incapacity and decrepitude.

It is a well known aspect of the Prophet's biography that he was well built and could throw a wrestler, was capable of traveling great distances without tiring, and fully conditioned to bear the hardships of armed struggle in the way of jihad. It is then quite bizarre to find people arguing that emaciation and gauntness are signs of true piety. The Hindus were the first to give currency to this belief, followed by the monastic Christians. In the end, it was the ignorant among the Sufis who brought the notion to Islam, giving rise to the belief that robust vitality is somehow a disgrace and implies some sort of corresponding deficiency in spirit. As if the sexually infirm and their like could rise to the rank of angels!

The Prophet Muhammad, upon him be peace, was the sublime exemplar and true to human nature in his beseeching the Lord to distance him from all calamity and illness. So, whenever a Muslim (in spite of his constant beseeching of the Lord in the manner of the Prophet) is beset by worldly troubles, he bears with them, and submits to the will of Allah, while repeating what the Prophet taught us to say at such a time:

Verily, unto Allah is what He takes, and unto Him is what He gives.

Or we may repeat what was taught in the Qur'an:

99

Verily, we are of Allah. And verily, unto Him shall we return. (al Baqarah 2: 15)

Secondly, the Prophet, upon him be peace, openly declared his dislike for poverty, debt and similar troubles which confound the normal state of affairs and lead to degradation. In my opinion, it is the height of folly to call people to poverty in the name of Allah and Islam. The difference between sufficiency and undue excess is well defined; though the definition of sufficiency itself may differ from person to person. The important thing is that the Prophet, upon him be peace, would ask his Lord, as documented in the hadith literature, for a life of stability, regular sustenance, and good deeds. Furthermore, he would often repeat this Qur'anic *du'a*:

O Lord! Grant us good in this world and good in the life to come, and keep us safe from suffering in the Fire. (al Baqarah 2: 201)

Yet, if he was ever besieged, or called upon to do battle, he endured deprivation resolutely without losing his good nature or sense of judgment. When plenty came his way, he gladly shared it with others. And it is well known that he had no real worldly possessions of his own. His own condition was rather the contrary, as this *du'a* sums up:

«اَللّٰهُمَّ اجْعَلْ حُبَّكَ أَحَبَّ إِلَيَّ مِنْ نَفْسِيْ، وَأَهْلِي، وَمَالِي، وَوَلَدِي، وَمِنَ الْمَاءِ الْبَارِدِ عَلَى الظَّمَأِ».

O Allah! Make love of You dearer to me than my self, my family, my wealth and my offspring; and dearer to me than cool water to a thirsty wayfarer.

Thirdly, the attitude of those who show dislike for those above them in life, and contempt for those below. Sadly, this kind of person can be found in all walks of life. The Prophet, upon him be peace, explicitly stated that he could have nothing to do with any such person:

He is not one of us who shows no respect for our elders, or who has no compassion for our young, or who has no appreciation for the rights of our learned.

The noble Prophet, upon him be peace, met everyone in the same spirit. Most certainly, he had no desire to be a tyrant on earth or a king over men; nor did he ever entertain ambitions of personal grandeur. On the contrary, what he desired was for Allah to deliver him from the arrogance of the ignorant, and from the injustice of aggressors. He frequently sought refuge in Allah from trials, envy, treachery, ignorance, all those things that detract from the dignity of a human being. Nonetheless, he was able to and did accept abuse and insults from others for the sake of his attachment to the Lord. What concerned him above all was that he should never become the object of the Almighty's wrath. In his prayers he would often say:

$$\text{«..إِنْ لَمْ يَكُ بِكَ عَلَيَّ غَضَبٌ فَلَا أُبَالِي، وَلَكِنْ عَافِيَتَكَ أَوْسَعُ لِي».}$$

If Your wrath be not upon me, I worry not. But Your favor would be far more liberal.

Let us here affirm the right of the Prophet, upon him be peace, to have us seek blessings for him. What exactly does it mean to seek blessings for him? It means our seeking mercy for him, combined with praise of him. The believers are to beseech Allah to favor their Prophet with higher standing and greater precedence, in return for all that he did for them, and all that he struggled for. Allah Himself has commended us to bless the Prophet and has informed us, praised be His name, that He and His angels bless the Prophet and the believers: it is written in the Qur'an. Then, what is the meaning of all these blessings?

The obvious meaning of blessings for the believers is the success and fruition of their efforts, their receiving divine assistance to change confusion, wandering, anxiety, deprivation, to plenty, enlightenment, uprightness; all of these spring from the mercy and bounty of the Lord, as this verse makes clear:

> He it is who bestows His blessings upon you, with His angels, so that He might take you out of the depths of darkness into the light. And, indeed, a dispenser of grace is He unto the believers. On the day when they meet Him, they will be welcomed with the greeting 'Peace'; and He will have prepared for them a most excellent reward. (al Ahzab 33: 43-44)

The reward will be increased for the afflicted believers who, though subjected to trial through their possessions or their lives, have not been shaken in their belief, in their devotion to Allah, but have remained firm in their commitment to Him through self surrender, and who acknowledge that their ultimate return is unto Him:

> It is they upon whom their Lord's blessings are bestowed, and it is they, they who are on the right path. (al Baqarah 2: 157)

If such attention is to be received by the steadfast believers, then what of the one responsibile for planting the seeds of faith, standing over them, repelling the attacks of men and Satan alike, dedicting his entire life to this single cause? Indeed, the Prophet's only concern was for mankind's enlightenment and guidance, as his only pleasure was to see people regularly involving themselves in the proper worship of Allah. The heavenly hosts follow his efforts in admiration, wondering how one man, in the frailty of his single human form, is able to defeat so many enemies, to erase their culture, and to establish the state of *tawhid* (divine unity) and the community of Islam. That is the meaning of Allah's saying:

> Verily, Allah and His angels bless the Prophet: (hence) O you who have attained to the faith, bless him and give yourselves up (to his guidance) in utter self surrender. (al Ahzab 33: 56)

Thus, our asking the Lord to bless him is affirmation of, and support for, his mission, devotion to his person, and a form of greeting of love and reverence. It is the binding force between the leader and his army, or the master and his followers, in obedience to the Almighty, commitment to His way, and abiding to it to the very end. In the same way, everything in creation is bound to the Creator, and participates in glorifying Allah and praying to Him:

> Are you not aware that it is Allah whose limitless glory all that are in the heavens and on earth extol, even the birds as they spread out their wings? Each (creature) knows indeed how to pray unto Him and glorify Him; and Allah has full knowledge of all that they do. (al Nur 24: 41)

It is preferable to use those lucid, yet simply worded blessings for the Prophet which have been passed down to us by the first generations of Muslims, rather than the affected, abstruse formulas for which missals have been written, group recitations convened, and names for the Prophet invented — names for which Allah has revealed no legitimation. Surely it is not the mere repetition of eloquent phrases that is important. What matters is one's acknowledgment of the favor done by the Prophet, upon him be peace, for the betterment of the believers, one's appreciation of the jihad he waged against the forces of ignorance, and one's allegiance to the nation which he founded in the name of ultimate truth.

This is the real meaning of seeking blessings for the Prophet of Allah, upon him be peace. And only those who give practical evidence of their appreciation of this meaning will receive the rewards promised to those who seek blessings for the Prophet, upon him be peace. Certainly those self acclaimed 'lovers of the Prophet' who hollowly echo set phrases, yet who are unable to stand in defense of the Sunnah, cannot ever be eligible for such rewards. It is with regard to the defenders of the faith, those who truly appreciate the Prophet, upon him be peace, that this hadith is related:

103

Whosoever seeks blessings for me will be blessed ten times over by the Almighty. 'Abd Allah ibn Mas'ud related that the Prophet, upon him be peace, said:

On the Day of Judgment, the people most deserving of (a relationship with) me will be those who have most often sought blessings for me.

Abu Hurayrah related that the Prophet, upon him be peace, said:

Do not make my grave a place of festivity; and seek blessings for me. For verily your blessings reach me no matter where you may happen to be when you seek them.

Of course, the spirit world has rules of its own which are far beyond the comprehension of mortals here in the material world. Suffice it to say that our blessings reach him with the greatest facility. We need not delve into the question of how this is accomplished.

In what we have read of the *du'as* of the Prophet, upon him be peace, we see that he spared no breath in asking forgiveness for himself. Even the Qur'an, in absolving him from sin, attributes it to him by the implication (that he needed absolution). What possible meaning can this have? What can he possibly have done that he should have to ask forgiveness for it?

We shall answer these questions calmly. There can be no doubt that Muhammad's page on the Book of Deeds is the most immaculate of all. This is true in spite of our not knowing of anyone who was more closely observed in his youth and old age, his waking and sleeping hours, or his public and private affairs. What, if anything, did his enemies say about him that might have led to his disgrace, or detracted from his honor? Nothing. Indeed, the most that his enemies could say about him was that the blows he aimed against falsehood have continued to echo over the centuries, and that no one, past or present, has ever presented to mankind a program of more perfect worship. Not even by way of calumny were any of the misdeeds attributed to the other Prophets, quite falsely, by the Bible writers like drunkenness, murder, adultery, incest and deception ever attributed to the Prophet of Islam.

Then what was the reason for the Prophet's seeking forgiveness? Let us begin by realizing that the differences between one person and the next may be very great indeed. It is only natural that certain individuals are possessed of greater physical or intellectual powers than others. As a general rule, then, the individual's success or failure, progress or decline, is determined in some relation to the natural ability with which he or she is endowed.

Since human beings are not equal insofar as their resolution, intellectual perceptions and overall capabilities are concerned, their accountability before Allah must be proportionate to their natural ability. Thus, what is accepted of one may be rejected in the case of another. Indeed, owing to this disparity, what might be seen as a good deed, coming from one man, might be considered a misdeed, coming from another. In this regard the well known saying was coined:

> The best deeds of the pious may well be the worst deeds of those most intimate.

It is a matter of ordinary experience that something that might be acceptable, or at least tolerable, coming from an ordinary person might be the greatest of insults coming from an extremely clever one.

Thus, we may say that what is sometimes attributed to the Prophets of Allah as sin is in reality 'sin' only in relation to the elevated positions which they held. Their 'sins' were certainly not of the order of those committed by ordinary men.

The great Egyptian scholar Mahmud 'Abbas al 'Aqqad once wrote, in an essay on literary standards, that under certain circumstances one should look not at what is said, but at who has said it. (In contravention of the general rule that would have one look at what is said or written, rather than at who has said or written it.)

'Aqqad's observation is a good one. It would be the height of folly to suppose that the Prophets committed the same kind of errors as ordinary people do. What they seek forgiveness for is undoubtedly something else, something more in keeping with their natural instinct for virtue. Even an ordinary individual, as he advances through different degrees of achievement, is bound to feel aghast when he looks back and considers how meager were his attainments then in relation to the present. It is at this point that he asks forgiveness of his Lord, and feels disdain for what he had done before, accounting his former deeds as repugnant and unworthy of himself in his present state. In the same way, the further the Prophet advanced in righteousness, and the more the signs of the Almighty were revealed to him, the more was his rapture in the praise and glorification of his Lord, and the greater his fervor in seeking His forgiveness.

Shortly, when we look at the Prophet Muhammad's worship and leadership, we shall see how he advanced from horizon to horizon as the verses of the Qur'an increased in number, as his struggle was carried forward phase after phase, and as the burden of the message he brought grew more and more onerous. The man who once addressed his clansmen from a hillock in Makkah, later went on to address his message to the rulers of vast empires; and the same man who debated with a mere handful of critics at the outset of his mission later mustered armies to fight the forces of ignorance and darkness. And for the sake of whom did he undertake these unceasing efforts? For Allah and no other.

From the beginning of his mission he spent nearly the whole night in worship, and he kept up long years in regular prayer and fasting. But did he ever stop to rest, as though his need had been satisfied? By no means. Rather, the more he accepted that he had been chosen by Allah for His message, the more he exhausted himself in the way of struggle and propagation. No wonder, then, that the following verses should have been revealed to him shortly before the fall of Makkah:

Verily We have laid open before you a manifest victory, so that Allah might show His forgiveness of all your faults, past as well as future, and thus bestow upon you the full measure of His blessings . . . (al Fath 48: 1-2)

The forgiveness referred to here is not for 'faults' committed or about to be committed. It is, rather, the communication of good tidings to the Soldier of the Lord that he has successfully completed his assigned mission, and that his feelings of unworthiness or inadequacy are only natural and, as such, should be accepted.

We are not speaking of sins in the ordinary sense, such as are committed by ordinary men, but the Prophet's perception, upon him be peace, that he has been somehow remiss in fulfilling his obligations to the Almighty, lax in the performance of his awesome duties. Thus Allah honored him with good tidings of 'forgiveness.' Indeed, when Allah says to His servant, 'I forgive you your sins, past as well as future,' it does not mean that the servant is excused from his duties, or that he is free to perform or neglect them as he pleases. Such an interpretation is obviously foolish. What is meant is that the servant has attained such a high degree of devotion that he will not be allowed to tumble, and that his future will be an extension of his present, in goodness and in the strength of his attachment to Allah.

The Prophet Muhammad, upon him be peace, was promised this kind of all-encompassing forgiveness, and he, in turn, promised it to those who took part in the Battle of Badr. Likewise, 'Uthman ibn 'Affan was promised the same when he gave so much of his wealth to outfit the Muslim army for the Tabuk campaign which was called the Campaign of Hardship.

It is related in an authentic hadith that Allah promises this forgiveness to a repentant man who, immediately after commission of a sin, seeks the forgiveness of Allah:

My servant knows that he has a Lord who can forgive or punish him for his sins. Do, then, as you please; for I have forgiven you. (Bukhari)

The sense of the above is that Allah has inscribed for each repentant servant his due, or his description, based on the established condition which he had attained during his lifetime, and that He then registers it for him before his death; because Allah knows that that particular servant will never lapse again into error.

12

IS *DU'A* AN ORDINARY MEANS?

We could say that *du'a* is an ordinary means, if we suppose the matter to be no more than the weak asking for help from the powerful. When a boy asks his father to get him this or that, he is using the most convenient agent or causative factor, a loving father. Obviously, if left to his own devices, the boy would never be able to produce the desired object.

When the Prophets turned to Allah for protection against the injuries and insults of the disbelievers, their usual resource was a *du'a* as in this celebrated instance in the Qur'an:

> Long before those (who now deny resurrection) did Noah's people call it a lie, and they gave the lie to Our servant and said, 'Mad is he!' and he was repulsed. Thereupon he called out to his Lord, 'Verily, I am defeated; come to my aid!' And so We caused the gates of heaven to open with water pouring down in torrents, and caused the earth to burst forth with springs, so that the waters met for a purpose preordained. (al Qamar 54: 12)

However, our discussion here is not immediately concerned with this. What we do propose to consider are the *dhikr* and incantations, related in authentic hadith, which are to be recited by believers at specific times, or in the event of their being beset by difficulties which trouble them and cause them to seek the help of Allah.

In one such authentic hadith it is related that the Prophet of Allah, upon him be peace, would blow[1] on his hands, on getting into bed but before sleeping, recite the last two surahs of the Qur'an, and then run his hands over his entire body.

In another version of the same hadith, it is related that when the Prophet, upon him be peace, went to bed at night, he would clasp his hands together, and blow into them, and then recite Surat al Ikhlas and the last two surahs of the Qur'an, and then run his hands over as much as he could of his body, beginning with his head, face and the front of his body, repeating this three times.

The three surahs referred to mention *tawhid* or the Unity of God, and the purity of His person and attributes. In addition, they urge one toward divine providence, and away from the evils of body and mind.

We shall refer, in what follows, to a number of incantations or verbal formulas which may be resorted to by the Muslim for the purpose of curing disease. Obviously, these must have some connection with the realm of the Unknown, otherwise the secret of sufflation or repetition of certain words and phrases are matters which altogether defeat understanding.

I feel I must mention here some established medical facts which will themselves take us to the brink of the Unknown. Viruses, lethal or fatal to almost every organism they come into contact with, are observed to have no effect on certain people, who have either developed or naturally possess, a resistance to that particular strain, no matter how deadly. It can and does happen that a person can be the carrier of an extremely deadly micro organism for years without ever becoming ill because of it.

---

[1] According to the scholars, this blowing or sufflation is merely a gentle expiration without the emission of moisture.

How is this so? And how is it that these micro organisms are stripped of their virulence?

We Muslims would answer: 'Of course, Allah! Who else?' In relation to the realm of the Unknown, the measured, physical world is so small as to be insignificant. And while it is within our abilities to treat many diseases, the greater portion still remains beyond them. Remedy by medicine is certainly effective. Indeed, the Prophet himself, upon him be peace, prescribed medicines, and various foods and drinks, as cures for disease. Nonetheless, after all is said and done, there still remains one final authority which makes a disease dormant or active, infectious or non-infectious. Therefore, *du'a*, prayer to the Lord above, remains the force that it is. Should He will, the disease will take its course. And should He will, it will amount to nothing, and vanish without a trace.

In the light of the above, we shall now attempt to understand the efficacy of some of the remedies related in the hadiths.

It is related that 'Uthman ibn Abi al 'As complained of pain to the Prophet, upon him be peace, who told him: 'Put your hand on that part of your body which is painful, and say *Bismillah* three times, and seven times:

$$\text{«أَعُوذُ بِعِزَّةِ اللهِ، وَقُدْرَتِهِ مِنْ شَرِّ مَا أَجِدُ، وَأُحَاذِرُ».}$$

"I seek refuge in the honor of Allah and His power from the evil which find and watch out for."

It is related that Anas said to Thabit, may Allah have mercy on both of them, 'May I incant for you the incantation of the Prophet, upon him be peace?' When Thabit had assented, Anas repeated:

$$\text{«اللَّهُمَّ رَبَّ النَّاسِ، مُذْهِبَ الْبَاسِ، إِشْفِ أَنْتَ}$$
$$\text{الشَّافِي، لَا شَافِيَ إِلَّا أَنْتَ، شِفَاءً لَا يُغَادِرُ سَقَماً».}$$

'O Lord, Lord of mankind. Remover of difficulties, cure me, for You are the Curer — there is no curer other than You — with such a cure as will never be followed by illness.'

I should like to pause here to consider an interesting event, as related by Imam Bukhari in his collection of authentic hadith, on the authority of Abu Sa'id al Khudri:

A group of the Companions of the Prophet of Allah were on a journey, and had stopped at a bedouin settlement in the hope of being received as guests. The bedouins, however, refused to have them. Shortly thereafter, the bedouin chief was bitten (by a snake or a scorpion), and the tribe did all they could to save him, but to no avail. Then they decided among themselves to approach the travellers to see if they might have something which might be of use.

So they went to them and said, 'Listen, O band of travellers! Our chief has been bitten, and nothing we do for him seems to help. Perhaps one of you has something?' Then one of the travellers said, 'By Allah, I can cure him. But, by Allah, we had asked to be received as guests and you refused. So I will not cure him until you have made us an offer.'

So they agreed upon a number of goats and the man went to the chief, and sufflated, and then recited the opening chapter of the Qur'an over him. It was as if the man had been released from his bonds (as a camel is released), so that he got up and walked away without the least discomfort. Then the bedouins gave them all that they had agreed upon.

Some of the Muslims said, 'Distribute the goats.' But the one who had done the incantation said, 'No, not until we have consulted the Prophet of Allah, upon him be peace, in the matter, and seen what he decides.'

So, on their return, they went to the Prophet, upon him be peace, and told him their story. The Prophet, upon him be peace, said to the one who had recited the Opening Surah over the sick man, 'How did you know that it would cure him?' Then he said, 'You have done well. Distribute the goats, and set aside a share for me as well.' Then the Prophet laughed at all that had occurred.

In a similar version of the same hadith, the Prophet, upon him be peace, is reported to have said,

'Eat up! Because, for the life of me, so many consume the wages of black magic, whereas you will eat from the magic of the Truth.'

This is a story which, for many reasons, has never failed to arrest my attention. The Opening Surah of the Holy Book is certainly of great importance for its praise of the Almighty and for the *du'a* it contains. But I had always supposed that its benefit was limited to the one reciting it. Yet this story showed me that it could also benefit one for whom it was especially recited.

The story tells us that the party of travellers from among the Companions of the Prophet camped near a tribe who refused to accept them as guests. Among the bedouin Arabs, in particular, this kind of behaviour is so ignoble as to be unspeakable. For myself, I think they behaved no less out of miserliness than out of dislike for Islam, and for those who embraced it. By the will of Allah something poisonous bit the tribal chieftain and left him in such helpless agony that his people were compelled to turn to the Prophet's Companions for help. Most remarkably, the one who actually treated the sick man by performing the incantation of the Opening Surah was the first to hesitate about taking the negotiated fee, and to doubt its permissibility. Indeed, his behavior indicated that he was a man who combined true faith with extreme prudence. And that is the crucial point. For not every incanter is a healer, and not every incantation is a cure. Yet Allah has servants who, when they will, He wills; and when they call down His bounty, it comes.

The Prophet, upon him be peace, was pleased with the whole affair, and desired to please the incanter. So he joined the group in partaking of the fee. And why should he not be pleased at the result produced by Revelation accompanied by complete faith and good deeds!

It is impossible to deny the element of the Unknown in this story. And equally impossible to generalize its application regarding people of higher or lesser spiritual merit, those who maintain firm relationships with the Almighty and those who attribute themselves to Him only through the weakest of connections. The most successful of the pious surely derive their physical well being and their resistance to disease and pain from the gushing spring within their hearts, drawing upon the pardon of Allah and His vitality.

We return to the most pious of all, Muhammad ibn 'Abd Allah, upon him be peace, to relate that he used to overcome all temporary complaints by turning to Allah and seeking refuge in Him. At this point someone might argue: We know of his physical well being and strength, and that he was endowed in this regard with what no other has ever been endowed. How is it that he should be beset with illness or infirmities which caused him to seek refuge in Allah?

Our answer is that the Last of the Prophets, upon him be peace, was indeed endowed with exceptional physical and intellectual powers in order to assist him in the most onerous mission ever undertaken. But his nightly vigils in *tahajjud* prayer and recitation of the Qur'an, his daily exertion in worship and labor, in unending jihad, in bearing the problems of others, and all of this continuously for a full quarter century, increasing all the while and never subsiding, in addition to an amazingly light ration of food and drink — all of these factors contributed to wearing down his sturdy body and its decline in health.

I have studied the lives of a number of leaders and found them to consume great quantities of stimulants and restoratives, not to mention food and drink. While in the biography of Muhammad, upon him be peace, I find it recorded that he was once in need of nourishment, and so vinegar was brought to him, as there was nothing else. The Prophet dipped whatever crusts of bread he had in the vinegar and said, 'Vinegar, what a fine condiment!' While, on other days, perhaps, he found nothing at all to eat, so that he fasted from before sunrise to sunset.

What body could bear, in spite of such deprivation, the hardships of struggle against the idolators, and of giving training and education to a generation of desert Arabs destined to illumine the globe? Surely, behind this extraordinary steadfastness and endurance, was a great deal of spiritual succour, sent from on high, through the *dhikr* of Allah.

In an authentic hadith it is related that whenever the Prophet, upon him be peace, had a physical complaint, he would recite over himself the last two chapters of the Qur'an and sufflate. Imam Zuhri, one of the narrators of this hadith, was asked how the sufflation was performed. He answered that the Prophet, upon him be peace, would blow into his hands and then rub his face with them. The Prophet, upon him be peace, continued this practice throughout his lifetime. In another hadith it is related that he, upon him be peace, recited and sufflated in his final illness. Said 'A'ishah, may Allah be pleased with her, 'When it became too much for him to bear, I recited and sufflated over him myself; but I used his own hand to rub him with, for the sake of *barakah*.' That is, 'A'ishah, may Allah be pleased with her, would take the Prophet's hand in her own, and rub it over his body in the confidence that more blessings would issue from his hand.

This was the Prophet's personal physician in the world of mortals, where every leader has his own personal physician! In this way, the Prophet, upon him be peace, used to overcome his illnesses, until he took his final repose with the Almighty.

My references, earlier in this chapter, to the realm of the Unknown were made in relation to the perceptive faculties of the ordinary person. This is because, generally, we see only the shadows of reality, as reality itself is nearly permanently obscured by our personal longings and desires, even in spite of an admixture of faith and sincerity. However, in relation to the Prophets, peace be upon them all, the matter is not as it is with us. Rather, theirs is a witnessing which places their perception of the Lord of creation before the perception of creation itself.

The Prophet of Prophets, upon him be peace, possessed a spirituality of tremendous proportions, the divine radiance of which never diminished. It was his mission to ever strive for the betterment of those around him, and to overcome their materialism with his purity and effulgence. This now prompts us to take a brief look at the pillars of Islam; to see how they can become the stairway to spiritual progress, and the source of constant remembrance of Allah. And to see, further, how the Prophet, upon him be peace, was unique in performing them.

13

FUNDAMENTALS OF WORSHIP

When the Prophet, upon him be peace, began his prayer, he would
first recite the following:

«اللَّهُ أَكْبَرُ كَبِيراً وَالْحَمْدُ لِلَّهِ كَثِيراً وَسُبْحَانَ اللَّهِ بُكْرَةً
وَأَصِيلاً، وَجَّهْتُ وَجْهِيَ لِلَّذِي فَطَرَ السَّمَوَاتِ
وَالأَرْضَ حَنِيفاً مُسْلِماً وَمَا أَنَا مِنَ الْمُشْرِكِينَ. إِنَّ
صَلاتِي وَنُسُكِي وَمَحْيَايَ وَمَمَاتِي لِلَّهِ رَبِّ الْعَالَمِينَ، لاَ
شَرِيكَ لَهُ وَبِذَلِكَ أُمِرْتُ وَأَنَا أَوَّلُ الْمُسْلِمِينَ».

Allah is the greatest in the greatest measure; and the fullest
praise to Allah and glory be to Allah, early and late!

(As a true Muslim,) I direct my attention toward the One
who created the heavens and earth, and I am not one of the
idolators. Verily my prayer, my devotion, my life and my
death are for Allah, Lord of the Worlds. He has no partner.
That is what I have been charged with, and I am the first
among Muslims.

«اللَّهُمَّ أَنْتَ الْمَلِكُ لاَ إِلَهَ إِلاَّ أَنْتَ، أَنْتَ رَبِّي وَأَنَا
عَبْدُكَ. ظَلَمْتُ نَفْسِي، وَاعْتَرَفْتُ بِذَنْبِي فَاغْفِرْ لِي
ذُنُوبِي جَمِيعاً لاَ يَغْفِرُ الذُّنُوبَ إِلاَّ أَنْتَ. وَاهْدِنِي

لِإحْسَنِ الْأَخْلَاقِ لَا يَهْدِي لِإحْسَنِهَا إلَّا أَنْتَ،
وَاصْرِفْ عَنِّي سَيِّئَهَا لَا يَصْرِفُ سَيِّئَهَا إلَّا أَنْتَ».

O Allah, You are the Sovereign, there is no god but You. You
are my Lord and I am Your slave. I have done injustice to
myself, and admit my wrong, so forgive me all my sins. No
one but You can forgive sins. And guide me to the finest
morality. No one can guide me to the finest morality but You.
And divert the worst of it away from me. No one can divert
the worst of it but You.

«لَبَّيْكَ وَسَعْدَيْكَ، وَالْخَيْرُ كُلُّه فِي يَدَيْكَ، وَالشَّرُّ لَيْسَ إلَيْكَ،
أَنَا بِكَ وَإلَيْكَ، تَبَارَكْتَ وَتَعَالَيْتَ، اَسْتَغْفِرُكَ وَأَتُوبُ إلَيْكَ. !!».

l am present and ready to obey. All good is in Your hands,
and evil is not of You. I am of You and (will return) unto You.
You are blessed and exalted. I seek Your forgiveness and
unto You I repent.

The meaning of 'and evil is not of You' is that Allah does not intro-
duce evil into the life of a servant, but that the servant brings it upon
himself through his misdeeds.

Whatever calamity befalls you is an outcome of what your
own hands have wrought, although He pardons much. (al
Shura 42: 30)

Alternatively, the Prophet, upon him be peace, sometimes began his
prayer with the following:

«اَللّهُمَّ بَاعِدْ بَيْنِي وَبَيْنَ خَطَايَايَ كَمَا بَاعَدْتَ بَيْنَ الْمَشْرِقِ
وَالْمَغْرِبِ. اَللّهُمَّ نَقِّنِي مِنْ خَطَايَايَ كَمَا يُنَقَّى الثَّوْبُ الْأَبْيَضُ مِنَ
الدَّنَسِ، اللّهُمَّ اغْسِلْنِي مِنْ خَطَايَايَ بِالْمَاءِ والثَّلْجِ وَالْبَرَدِ».

O Allah! Distance me from my sins as You have distanced the East from the West. O Allah! Cleanse me of my sins as a white cloth is cleansed of dirt. O Allah! Wash me of my sins with water, ice and cold.

And sometimes he, upon him be peace, would begin:

«سُبْحَانَكَ اَللّٰهُمَّ وَبِحَمْدِكَ، وَتَبَارَكَ اسْمُكَ، وَتَعَالَى جَدُّكَ، وَلَا إِلٰهَ غَيْرُكَ...».

Glory be to You, O Lord, and praise. Blessed is Your name, and exalted is Your state. There is no god but You.

When he, upon him be peace, assumed the bowing position in prayer, he would say:

«اَللّٰهُمَّ لَكَ رَكَعْتُ، وَبِكَ آمَنْتُ، وَلَكَ أَسْلَمْتُ، خَشَعَ لَكَ سَمْعِي، وَبَصَرِي، وَمُخِّي، وَعَظْمِي، وَعَصَبِي».

O Lord, for You I have made *ruku'* and in You I have placed my faith, and to You I have committed myself. My ears, my eyes, my marrow, and my sinews have humbled themselves before you.

When he raised himself from the bowing position, he would say:

«سَمِعَ اللّٰهُ لِمَنْ حَمِدَهُ، رَبَّنَا لَكَ الْحَمْدُ، حَمْداً كَثِيراً طَيِّباً مُبَارَكاً فِيهِ، مِلْءَ السَّمٰوَاتِ، وَمِلْءَ الْأَرْضِ، وَمِلْءَ مَا بَيْنَهُمَا، وَمِلْءَ مَا شِئْتَ مِنْ شَيْءٍ بَعْدُ.. أَهْلَ الثَّنَاءِ وَالْمَجْدِ، أَحَقُّ مَا قَالَ الْعَبْدُ وَكُلُّنَا لَكَ عَبْدٌ لَا

مَانِعَ لِمَا أَعْطَيْتَ، وَلَا مُعْطِيَ لِمَا مَنَعْتَ، وَلَا يَنْفَعُ ذَا
الْجَدِّ مِنْكَ الْجَدُّ».

May Allah listen to those who praise Him. O Lord, may Your praises fill the heavens, and fill the earth, and fill everything between them, and fill whatever else remains to be filled after that.

You alone are deserving of praise and majesty. The most truthful thing any servant ever said (and we are all Your servants) is: there is no one to withhold what You give, and no one to give what You withhold. And no wealthy person's wealth will avail him with You. [That is, that no manner of wealth or property which You have given to someone will be of any benefit to him. Rather, it is only his deeds which will be accounted when he meets You for the final reckoning.]

When he assumed the *sajdah* prostration position, he would say, upon him be peace:

«سُبْحَانَ ذِي الْجَبَرُوتِ وَالْمَلَكُوتِ وَالْكِبْرِيَاءِ،
وَالْعَظَمَةِ».

Glory to the Possessor of might, of sovereignty, of majesty and of greatness.

«اَللَّهُمَّ أَعُوذُ بِرِضَاكَ مِنْ سَخَطِكَ، وَبِمُعَافَاتِكَ مِنْ
عُقُوبَتِكَ وَأَعُوذُ بِكَ مِنْكَ، سُبْحَانَكَ! لَا أُحْصِيْ ثَنَاءً
عَلَيْكَ، أَنْتَ كَمَا أَثْنَيْتَ عَلَى نَفْسِكَ».

O Lord, I seek refuge in Your pleasure from Your wrath, and in Your forgiveness from Your punishment, and in You from You. Glory be to You! I am incapable of counting Your praises. You are as You have praised Yourself.

120

As I read these lines I cannot help but feel that all the Prophets, upon them be peace, and the heavenly hosts as well, have arranged themselves in lines behind the Prophet Muhammad, upon him be peace, as he recites the *du'a* which Allah inspires his heart and tongue to utter. I wonder, is there an element among the many elements of worship, or of desire and fear of the Lord, which escaped Muhammad, upon him be peace, while he was thus engaged in prayer? Did any of the angels of the heavenly hosts, or the blessed Prophets of Allah, ever greet the Lord of the Worlds with a greeting purer and more sincere than Muhammad's, or praise Him with praise more sublime, or beg His pardon for shortcomings[1] in a more sensitive and befitting manner?

In worship of Allah, through seeking knowledge of Him and giving thanks unto Him, we see a unique individual, one striding so far ahead of his fellow men that they seem to be but at the crawling stage, so to speak, and gasping for breath to keep up, while in their ears there echoes the continually exhilarating sound of a man praising and glorifying Allah. And who is this man, so immersed in the worship of Allah; who is this returning and repentant one? Indeed, it is Muhammad ibn 'Abd Allah, upon him be peace.

But, when we turn and descend from this pinnacle, we still hear the hissing of the prevaricators: 'Muhammad was not a prophet.' We have heard baseless claims from them before, when they have alleged: 'God has a son, and His son is also God.' Greater is their misfortune! There is no god but Allah, and Muhammad is the Prophet of Allah!

Prayer is the second pillar of Islam. This is not, however, the place to go into the details of how to perform salah. As to the *du'a* and *dhikr* cited above, it should be understood that they are not *wajib* or

---

[1] Shortcoming, here, can have but one of two possible meanings; either that a man's ability is limited, whereas his duty is awesome; or that the Majesty of the Lord is so far beyond comprehension that no words may adequately express it, or do it justice.

necessary elements of salah, as salah may be completed with far simpler and briefer prayers and recitations. Our purpose in citing them was merely to direct attention to the sure skill and fullness of Muhammad, upon him be peace, in *dhikr* and *du'a*.

In nearly every religion, prayer is considered the foremost form of worship. It was the foremost preoccupation of the Prophet of Islam, upon him be peace. Indeed, he made it a sign of heedfulness, a token of submission and captivation, and a mark of absolute allegiance to Allah, Lord of the Worlds. But there can be no prayer if it is accompanied by faulty understanding, or refusal to submit to the will of the Almighty. Thus, it is *kufr* (disbelief) to imagine that there is more than one possessor of divinity, or to rebel against Allah's commandments.

There are places and ways of worship for each of the various religions. Islam, however, teaches that worship is exclusively for the One, true God, that succour is to be sought from the One God, and that the ultimate return of all creation is unto that same One God. The Prophet Muhammad, upon him be peace, was the finest person ever to acquaint mankind with the One God, to evoke in them love for Him, and to impart to them the knowledge that their Lord is more merciful to them than a parent to its child, and more caring than the most intimate companion.

I have explained on other occasions that the Islamic way of instruction is to combine attributes of awesomeness and attraction. In fact, man cannot do without this combination. The world is full of Pharaohs seduced into tyranny through the exercise of power, beggars in need of aid, and people gone astray in search of guidance.

In the following Qur'anic verse there is something for each group.

> Verily, Your Lord's grip is exceedingly strong! Behold, it is He who creates in the first instance, and He it is who will bring forth anew. And He alone is Truly Forgiving, All Embracing in His love, in sublime almightiness enthroned. (al Buruj 85: 12-15)

Those aspects of the mission of Muhammad which evoke love for the Almighty, and establish within the hearts of men love for one another are as an all engulfing flood, unparalleled in history.

When a problem confronts us, and we are unable to decide how to resolve it, should we not turn to Allah? Ask Him to set us in the right direction? After all, no one can be closer to us than He is. So why do we ignore Him? It is related on the authority of Jabir ibn 'Abd Allah that the Prophet, upon him be peace, used to teach his Companions to seek, through a special *du'a*, Allah's guidancein all matters which affected them. He said, upon him be peace: 'When you are confused about what you should do in a certain situation, then pray two *rak'at* of *nafl salah* (supererogatory prayer) and read the following *du'a*:

بِسْمِ اللّٰهِ الرَّحْمٰنِ الرَّحِيْمِ

«اَللّٰهُمَّ إِنِّي أَسْتَخِيْرُكَ بِعِلْمِكَ، وَأَسْتَقْـدِرُكَ بِقُدْرَتِكَ، وَأَسْأَلُكَ مِنْ فَضْلِكَ الْعَظِيْمِ، فَإِنَّكَ تَقْدِرُ وَلَا أَقْدِرُ، وَتَعْلَمُ وَلَا أَعْلَمُ وَأَنْتَ عَلَّامُ الْغُيُوبِ. اَللّٰهُمَّ إِنْ كُنْتَ تَعْلَمُ أَنَّ هٰذَا الْأَمْرَ خَيْرٌ لِّيْ فِيْ دِيْنِيْ وَمَعَاشِيْ، وَعَاقِبَةِ أَمْرِيْ عَاجِلِ أَمْرِيْ وَآجِلِهِ، فَاقْدِرْهُ لِيْ، ثُمَّ بَارِكْ لِيْ فِيْهِ. وَإِنْ كُنْتَ تَعْلَمُ أَنَّ هٰذَا الْأَمْرَ شَرٌّ فِيْ دِيْنِيْ وَمَعَاشِي وَعَاقِبَةِ أَمْرِي وَعَاجِلِ أَمْرِي وَآجِلِهِ فَاصْرِفْهُ عَنِّي وَاصْرِفْنِي عَنْهُ، وَاقْدِرْ لِيَ الْخَيْرَ حَيْثُ كَانَ، ثُمَّ رَضِّنِي بِهِ».

O Allah, I ask You, of Your knowledge, for guidance and of Your power, for strength; and I ask You of Your excessive generosity. Certainly You are powerful and I am not, and You are the Knower of the unknown. O Allah, if You know this matter (here the supplicant should substitute for the words, 'this matter' whatever it is specifically that he has in mind, for example, this journey, or marriage, etc.) to be good for my religion, my worldly life, my life in the next world, my present state of affairs or my future state, then decree it for me and make it easy, and bless me in it. And if You know this matter to be detrimental to my religion, my worldly life, my life in the next world, my present state of affairs or my future state, then divert it from me, and turn me away from it, and decree for me that which is good, wherever it may be. And then make me to be pleased with it.

I am astounded at Muhammad's enemies who derisively say that Allah is a high-handed oppressor. My reply to them is: Be it so; who else could bring low the tyrants of the earth, if not the Almighty? And who, other than the Majestic, could efface their arrogance? Surely, the deliverance of this world from the clutches of tyranny would be a mercy conferred! And yet, the Chastiser of Tyrants can say to their broken subjects, 'I will mend you,' and to those in quest of the right way, 'I will guide you', and to those who seek good, 'Ask for the bounty of Allah. Surely Allah has knowledge of everything.'

And so, if ever you find yourself in need of anything, turn to Your Lord. It is written:

The exclusiveness of his creative Being is such that when He wills a thing to be, He but says unto it, 'Be' — and it is. (Ya Sin 36: 82)

It is related on the authority of 'Abd Allah ibn Abi Awfa that the Prophet of Allah, upon him be peace, said, 'Whoever among you has any kind of need, whether it be of Allah or of a human being, should perform *wudu'* (ablution) and two *rak'at* of salah (prayer). Then he should praise Allah and invoke His blessings on the Prophet, peace be upon him, and say the following *du'a*:

لَا إِلٰهَ إِلَّا اللّٰهُ الْحَلِيْمُ الْكَرِيْمُ، سُبْحَانَ اللّٰهِ رَبِّ الْعَرْشِ الْعَظِيْمِ وَالْحَمْدُ لِلّٰهِ رَبِّ الْعَالَمِيْنَ. أَسْأَلُكَ

مُوْجِبَاتِ رَحْمَتِكَ، وَعَزَائِمَ مَغْفِرَتِكَ وَالْغَنِيْمَةَ مِنْ كُلِّ
بِرٍّ، وَالسَّلَامَةَ مِنْ كُلِّ إِثْمٍ، لَاتَدَعْ لِي ذَنْباً إِلَّا
غَفَرْتَهُ، وَلَا هَمّاً إِلَّا فَرَّجْتَهُ، وَلَا حَاجَةً هِيَ لَكَ رِضاً
إِلَّا قَضَيْتَهَا يَا أَرْحَمَ الرَّاحِمِيْنَ».

There is no god but Allah, the Clement, the Generous. I celebrate the glory of Allah, Lord of the Magnificent Throne.
All praise be unto Allah, Lord of the Worlds. I seek of You
that which will make certain (for me) Your forgiveness, as
well as a share of every virtue, and freedom from every
offence. Do not leave me a wrong without relieving me of
it, or a need that meets with Your pleasure without providing for it. O Most Merciful of the Merciful.

At last, this world with all its joys and sorrows comes to an end, and
man returns to his Lord after completing his period of trial on earth.

As it was He who brought you into being in the first
instance, so also unto Him you will return: some of you He
will have graced with His guidance, whereas for some a
straying from the right path will have become unavoidable.
(al A'raf 7: 29-30)

The world becomes a collection of memories, and man then steps on
the threshold of the world to come.

Whenever a Muslim died in the Prophet's city (Madinah al Munaw-
warah) the Prophet, upon him be peace, would pray over him:

«اَللَّهُمَّ اغْفِرْ لَهُ وَارْحَمْهُ، وَعَافِهِ، وَاعْفُ عَنْهُ، وَأَكْرِمْ
نُزُلَهُ، وَوَسِّعْ مُدْخَلَهُ، وَاغْسِلْهُ بِالْمَاءِ وَالثَّلْجِ وَالْبَرَدِ،
وَنَقِّهِ مِنَ الْخَطَايَا كَمَا يُنَقَّى الثَّوْبُ الْأَبْيَضُ مِنَ

الدَّنَسِ، وَأَبْدِلْهُ دَاراً خَيْراً مِنْ دَارِهِ، وَأَهْلاً خَيْراً
مِنْ أَهْلِهِ، وَزَوْجاً خَيْراً مِنْ زَوْجِهِ، وَأَدْخِلْهُ الْجَنَّةَ
وَأَعِذْهُ مِنْ عَذَابِ الْقَبْرِ، وَمِنْ عَذَابِ النَّارِ.

O Allah, forgive and have mercy on him (or her). Grant him
ease and respite. Make his resting place a noble one, and
facilitate his entry. Cleanse him with water, snow and cool-
ness, and purify him of wrongdoing as a white cloth is puri-
fied of grime. Grant him an abode finer than his worldly
one, and grant him entrance to Paradise and protect him
from the chastisement of the grave, and protect him from the
chastisement of the Fire.

The narrator of the hadith in which the above funeral prayer was
recorded comments:

I wished that I could have been the one who had died so as
to have had this blessed prayer said at my funeral.

Of the Prophet's various funeral prayers, this is the one most
favoured by Imam Shafi'i:

«اَللّٰهُمَّ هَذَا عَبْدُكَ، وَابْنُ عَبْدِكَ خَرَجَ مِنْ رَوْحِ
الدُّنْيَا وَسَعَتِهَا وَمَحْبُوبِيْهَا وَأَحِبَّائِهِ فِيْهَا إلى ظُلْمَةِ
الْقَبْرِ، وَمَا هُوَ لَاقِيْهِ».
«كَانَ يَشْهَدُ أَنْ لَا إِلٰهَ إِلَّا أَنْتَ، وَأَنَّ مُحَمَّداً عَبْدُكَ
وَرَسُوْلُكَ وَأَنْتَ أَعْلَمُ بِهِ».
«اَللّٰهُمَّ إِنَّهُ نَزَلَ بِكَ وَأَنْتَ خَيْرُ مَنْزُوْلٍ بِهِ، وَأَصْبَحَ
فَقِيْراً إلى رَحْمَتِكَ وَأَنْتَ غَنِيٌّ عَنْ عَذَابِهِ، وَقَدْ جِئْنَاكَ
رَاغِبِيْنَ إِلَيْكَ، شُفَعَاءَ لَهُ».

«اَللَّهُمَّ إِنْ كَانَ مُحْسِناً فَزِدْ فِي إِحْسَانِهِ، وَإِنْ كَانَ
مُسِيئاً فَتَجَاوَزْ عَنْه. . وَآتِهِ بِرَحْمَتِكَ رِضَاكَ، وَقِهِ فِتْنَةَ
الْقَبْرِ وَعَذَابِهِ، وَافْسَحْ لَهُ فِي قَبْرِهِ، وَجَافِ الْأَرْضَ
عَنْ جَنْبَيْهِ، وَلَقِّهِ بِرَحْمَتِكَ الْأَمْنَ مِنْ عَذَابِكَ، حَتَّى
تَبْعَثَهُ إِلَى جَنَّتِكَ يَاأَرْحَمَ الرَّاحِمِينَ».

O Allah! This is Your slave, the son (or daughter) of Your slave, gone out from the ease of this world and its spaciousness, leaving behind both those he loved and those who loved him, for the darkness of the grave and whatever is in store for him. He used to give witness that there is no god but You, and that Muhammad is Your slave and Prophet, and You know all about him.

O Allah, now he has alighted at Your door, and You are the most generous of hosts; he has become as a beggar for Your mercy, and You have no need to punish him. We approach You as Your votaries, and as petitioners for him.

O Allah, if this man was indeed a doer of good, then increase him in his good. And if he did wrong, then overlook it, and, in Your mercy, show him Your pleasure, and protect him from the chastisement of the grave and its torments, until such a time as You take him into Your Garden, O Most Merciful of the Merciful!

For all believers, prayer (salah) is indeed a sacred duty linked to particular times of the day as indicated by the visible movements of the sun; before sunrise by about a hour and a half, after it has passed its noonday peak, at the mid afternoon descent, just after its setting, and after the disappearance of the post sunset red on the horizon. In the same way that the believers look toward the sun for the regulation of their daily worship, they look toward the moon for the regulation of their fasting and pilgrimage. Thus time, in more ways than one, is for the believer a mode of transition to the world to come.

The Prophet of Allah, upon him be peace, often drew the attention of his Companions to the sun and moon in all their resplendent glory, and told the believers that, in the next world, the beatific sight of their Lord would be granted them with equal clarity. Is it not befitting, then, that the believer should prepare for that meeting by doing as many good deeds as may ensure for him or her a handsome consequence?

The most important of all good deeds is to remember one's Lord, and never to be negligent of Him; to thank Him and never be ungrateful, and to never allow His creation to become as a veil before Him, or an obstacle in the way of performing one's duties to Him. The Prophet Muhammad, upon him be peace, was a true man of God in both his thoughts and his behavior, so that he took advantage of every opportunity to remember Allah, to greet Him, to express his love for Him, and to give witness to His oneness.

Thus, it is related on the authority of Ibn 'Umar that whenever the Prophet, upon him be peace, saw the new moon, he would say:

$$ \text{«اللهُ أَكْبَرُ، اللَّهُمَّ أَهِلَّهُ عَلَيْنَا بِالْيُمْنِ وَالإِيمَانِ} $$
$$ \text{وَالسَّلامَةِ وَالإِسْلامِ، وَالتَّوْفِيقِ لِمَا تُحِبُّ وَتَرْضَى،} $$
$$ \text{رَبُّنَا وَرَبُّكَ اللهُ».} $$

Allah is the Greatest! O Allah, let this moon rise above us in good fortune and faith, in peace and Islam, and in success in the achievement of that which is pleasing to, and loved by You! Our Lord, and the Lord of the moon is Allah!

In another narration it is related that he would say, upon him be peace:

وَهِلَالَ خَيْرٍ وَرُشْدٍ، هِلَالَ خَيْرٍ وَرُشْدٍ، هِلَالَ خَيْرٍ
وَرُشْدٍ. آمَنْتُ بِاللهِ. الَّذِي خَلَقَكَ، آمَنْتُ بِاللهِ
الَّذِي خَلَقَكَ، آمَنْتُ بِاللهِ الَّذِي خَلَقَكَ، الْحَمْدُ للهِ
الَّـذِي ذَهَبَ بِشَـهْـرِ . . . . وَجَـاءَ
بِشَهْرِ . . . .

A new moon of blessings and guidance! A new moon of
blessings and guidance! A new moon of blessings and guidance! I believe in Allah, the one that created you! (Thrice).
Praise to Allah who has taken away the month of . . . (name
the outgoing month)[2] and ushered in the month of . . . (name
the incoming month).[3]

Such is the heart of the true believer. A heart which beats in constant anticipation of the time appointed for the praising of the One
who changes night into day; which awaits with optimism the coming favor of the Lord and bids farewell to favors past. Time, to such
a believer, is a grant to be spent in the service of Allah. Thus, not a
moment of that ephemeral quantity is spent in negligence or frivo-
lity; but rather in prayer, in fasting, in jihad, and in unending effort
to lead mankind to (knowledge of) their Creator.

Whenever fasting is mentioned, most people think immediately of
the month of Ramadan, because Ramadan is the month of fasting.
But the Prophet of Allah, upon him be peace, used to fast so often
that some thought he was always fasting. The words of the *du'a* he
said, upon him be peace, when breaking his fasts, give an indication
of the kind of discomfort he underwent when fasting in the Arabian
summer with its scorching and shrivelling heat. On the authority of
Ibn 'Umar this *du'a* is recorded:

---

[2] Should name the outgoing month.
[3] Should name the incoming month.

129

«ذَهَبَ الظَّمَأُ، وَابْتَلَّتِ الْعُرُوقُ، وَثَبَتَ الأَجْرُ إِنْ
شَاءَ اللَّهُ».

Gone is the thirst, moist are the veins, and assured is the
reward, if it be the will of Allah!

Occasionally he would simply say, upon him be peace:

«اَللَّهُمَّ لَكَ صُمْتُ، وَعَلَى رِزْقِكَ أَفْطَرْتُ».

O Allah, for You have I fasted and, with what You have provided, do I break fast.

'Abd Allah said, 'I heard the Prophet of Allah, upon him be peace,
say, "The prayer of the one who fasts, at the time of his breaking fast,
will surely be answered."'

Ibn Mulaykah said, 'I heard 'Abd Allah, the narrator of this hadith,
break his fast with the following prayer:

«اَللَّهُمَّ إِنِّي أَسْأَلُكَ بِرَحْمَتِكَ الَّتِي وَسِعَتْ كُلَّ شَيْءٍ أَنْ
تَغْفِرَ لِي».

O Allah, I ask You of Your mercy which is all encompassing,
so forgive me.

On the subject of Hajj (the pilgrimage to Makkah), I once heard
someone, as if he were apologising for it, say that Allah tests us in
both what we can rationally understand and what we cannot, in
order to see our obedience. I asked him, 'Do you mean to say that
the rites of pilgrimage are irrational?' After a moment's timid
silence, the man answered, 'That is what I mean. And I give Allah
my obedience in everything that He requires me to do.'

My reply to him was to say that there are any number of things in this world which have nothing to do with reason in either a positive or negative way. Yet to describe these matters as irrational would be more than incorrect. For example, we write in our own Arabic language from right to left, whereas Western languages are written from left to right. Now these are matters which are never described as rational or irrational. Rather, they have simply been agreed upon by people, and certainly no one would even think to reproach another over such a matter. In a military parade, the troops are required to salute in a certain way. They may, for example, jerk their weapons up, twirl them to the left or right, place them on their shoulders and then turn their heads in the direction of the commander's review stand, and so forth. What is all this? Nothing more than convention, matters agreed upon and accepted by people. We may find these things agreeable or disagreeable according to our own personal dispositions. Yet they are in no way connected to issues of reason and logic.

Islam is unquestionably opposed to all that is irrational or unnatural. But it has no objection to matters of convention and accepted use unless these are used in the service of falsehood.

The man then asked me if I meant to say that the rites of pilgrimage were of this conventional, inexplicable nature.

'Yes,' I said.

'Then why,' he asked, 'does *tawaf* consist of exactly seven circumambulations?'

'A basic principle of logic, since we are discussing logic, is that a circular question is automatically inadmissible,' I said. Then I added, 'If the number of circumambulations was less, or more, the question would be the same. Why is your name 'Ali and not Rashid? The question leads nowhere, is circular, and requires no logical reply. Yet, in spite of all this, the rites of pilgrimage, all of them, are logical. Furthermore, each of them has its own rationale.'

I went on to explain to the man that it is the right of mankind to take pride in the remembrance of their heritage, and to preserve those memories by erecting around them walls of reverence and awe; especially where those memories pertain to their values and beliefs. Now the rites of pilgrimage are part of a glorious history, in addition to their being the keys to a treasury of effusive spirituality. For this reason the pilgrimage is counted among the five pillars of Islam.

And anyone who honors the symbols set up by Allah shall know that, verily, these symbols derive their value from the God consciousness in the believers' hearts. (al Hajj 22: 32)

Allow me to elaborate upon the foregoing. Why is it that every year pilgrims with hearts aflame and eyes aglow set out in caravans from every continent, by land, sea and air, in the direction of the Ancient Temple? As a matter of fact, that 'Temple' deserves that kind of esteem. After all, it was built by Ibrahim, the father of the Prophets, as a citadel of monotheism and a meeting place for the worshippers of the One True God. Indeed, after a life and death struggle with the forces of idolatry, Ibrahim emerged the victorious champion of monotheism. Then, in substantiation of that spiritual triumph, Ibrahim and his son, Isma'il erected the temple.

Behold, the first Temple ever set up for mankind was indeed the one at Bakkah; rich in blessing, and a source of guidance unto all the worlds, full of clear signs. It is the place whereupon Ibrahim once stood; and whoever enters it finds inner peace. Hence pilgrimage to the Temple is a duty owed to Allah by all people who are able to undertake it. And as for those who deny the truth, verily, Allah does not stand in need of anything in all the worlds. (Al 'Imran 3: 96-7)

Without a doubt, the world's first mosque deserves to be made the objective of one's travels, to be visited by those who wish to pay their respects. It is only fitting that every mosque built after it should face in its direction. This is why the Sacred Mosque at Makkah has been made the *qiblah* or direction of prayer for all Muslims.

Hence, from wherever you may come forth, turn your face in prayer towards the Sacred Mosque; and wherever you all may be, turn your faces towards it. (al Baqarah 2: 150)

There is still another historical aspect which attracts Muslims to the Sacred Mosque. At the time of its construction, this huge community of believers was no more than a dream, and this ultimate revelation no more than a fervent prayer. Ibrahim and Isma'il said:

O our Lord! Make us commit ourselves unto You, and make out of our offspring a community that shall commit itself to You, and show us the ways of worship, and accept our repentance. Surely, You alone are the Acceptor of Repentance, the Dispenser of Grace. O our Lord! Raise up from the midst of our offspring a prophet from among themselves who shall convey to them Your signs, and impart to them revelation as well as wisdom, and cause them to grow in purity. (al Baqarah 2: 128-9)

Undoubtedly it is we who are meant to be the committed offspring mentioned in this prayer; and Muhammad, upon him be peace, the Last of the Prophets, is our spiritual and cultural father. Is it surprising, then, that we should feel ourselves somehow attached to this Sacred Mosque, or that we should visit it whenever we find the means to do so? Indeed, what a glorious past it has had. Imagine the multitudes that have travelled long and hard for a glimpse of it, and for a chance to partake of its goodness and blessings.

The ways we observe the rites of the Temple are by circumambulating it and facing it in prayer. In circumambulation (*tawaf*) we place the Black Stone to our left side and circle the Temple seven times. As we walk around, we say, 'Glory be to Allah, and praise be to Allah, and there is no god but Allah, and Allah is the Greatest.' Of course, we pray to Allah for whatever we wish in this or the next world.

You will be committing no sin if (during the pilgrimage) you seek to obtain any bounty from your Lord. (al Baqarah 2: 198)

Before the Almighty, man is a mere beggar. And the treasuries of Allah are never exhausted.

Yet, according to certain Christian missionaries, Muslims' attachment to the Ka'bah, and especially to the Black Stone, is of a material nature! This assertion is self-evidently ridiculous, for the monotheism in the hearts of Muslims is of a degree of conviction unparalleled in this world. The cry of the pilgrim from the moment he or she begins is: 'Here I am, O Lord, here I am! Here I am, there is none that is a partner to You, here I am! Surely, all praise, all bounty is Yours, and all power. There is none that is a partner to You . . .'

Whenever the pilgrims ascend a hill, or descend into a valley, or meet another group of pilgrims, and whenever they are shaded by the quiet of the night or the calm of the ocean, the cry surges to become an uproar! At such times the pilgrim is possessed by the feeling that the entire universe is ringing out in harmony with his cry, as is related in the following hadith:

> When the pilgrim calls out 'Here I am, O Lord, here I am,' then everything on his right and everything on his left, including trees, stones, and clay even unto the ends of the earth call out as well.

Nor is it surprising that the universe, itself in constant praise of Allah, should harmonize with a person devoid of all self desire and on a pious journey whose only goal is Allah's pleasure. The Prophet, upon him be peace, would never travel without first praying:

«اَللّٰهُمَّ إِلَيْكَ تَوَجَّهْتُ، وَبِكَ اعْتَصَمْتُ، اكْفِنِي مَا أَهَمَّنِي وَمَالَا أَهْتَمُّ بِهِ. اَللّٰهُمَّ زَوِّدْنِي التَّقْوَى وَاغْفِرْ لِي ذَنْبِي، وَوَجِّهْنِي لِلْخَيْرِ أَيْنَمَا تَوَجَّهْتُ. اَللّٰهُمَّ أَنْتَ الصَّاحِبُ فِي السَّفَرِ، وَالْخَلِيفَةُ فِي الْأَهْلِ وَالْمَالِ وَالْوَلَدِ».

O Allah! Unto You have I directed myself, and by You have I protected myself. Then suffice me in all that concerns me and in all that I have not concerned myself with. O Allah! Provide me with heedfulness and forgiveness for my sins, and direct me to goodness regardless of the direction I set out in. O Allah! be my companion in my travels, and my guardian in my family, wealth, and children.

A pilgrim is one who dedicates himself to the sole purpose of worshipping Allah, who yearns for His pleasure, who aspires to earn His favor, and who lives in dread of His punishment. Thus everything that is in his body functions through the sensations of desire, longing and love. In fact, I know of no group of people more deserving of the mercy of Allah or His forgiveness than those who make the annual pilgrimage.

After circumambulation, it is customary for the pilgrim to run back and forth between the two mounds called Safa and Marwah. This rite is essentially a commemoration and a perpetuation of the feelings of trust in Allah which obtained in the hearts of Hajar, mother of Isma'il, and of Ibrahim the Prophet, upon all of whom be peace.

Indeed, absolute trust in Allah is a fine and rare quality too precious to be found permeating just any heart. Rather, no one but the most firm in his relationship with Allah, the most sensitive of his own dependence upon Him, is capable of such trust. At times when all hope of human aid has been severed, when one's means and abilities amount to nothing, when the depths of the soul are overwhelmed by desolation, then what remains save abiding trust in the Almighty? Indeed, at such times it is faith and faith only that can allay misgivings and assuage anxieties.

In my mind's eye, I follow Hajar as she looks to her thirsty child, then scrambles bewilderedly to and fro in search of heaven's succour. Of course, she trusted Allah. She had even said to Ibrahim as he was about to depart and leave her in that dry and desolate valley, 'Is this what Allah ordered you to do?' 'Yes,' he answered. And just as decisively, she responded: 'Then He will not allow us to go to waste.' And now here she is, face to face with the trial, awaiting the intervention of heaven. Heaven intervenes, the spring called Zamzam gushes from the desert floor, the valley becomes rich after ages of barrenness, and from the suckling infant grows a community of great numbers and untold wealth, amongst whom is born the last and greatest of the Prophets, upon them all be peace! Therefore is it accounted among the signs of Allah in the rites of pilgrimage, running between the two mounds of Safa and Marwah in imitation of the mother of Ismail as she strove with unfailing hope to catch a glimpse of the Unseen.

How pressing is the need of the would be believer for an appreciation of trust which can, of itself, bring plenty where there was paucity, honor where there was ignominy; and then (the need) to make of his relationship with the Almighty an esteemed reality. This is, perhaps, at least part of what is meant in the following verse:

> Behold, Safa and Marwah are among the symbols set up by Allah; and thus, no wrong does he who, having come to the Temple on pilgrimage or on a pious visit, strides to and fro between these two, for, if one does more good than one is bound to do behold, Allah is responsive to gratitude, All Knowing. (al Baqarah 2: 158)

According to historians, when Ibrahim, upon him be peace, left Hajar and her son to face an unknown fate in that remote wilderness, Satan appeared to him at the place (Mina) and said, 'Is one truly capable of abandoning his family to die of hunger and thirst in this manner! Return, and save your kin.' But Ibrahim, upon him be peace, pelted Satan with stones and went on his way, praying:

> Our Lord! I have had some of my offspring settle by Your Sacred House in a valley without any crops, our Lord, so that they may keep up prayer. Then make men's hearts fond of them, and provide them with fruits that they might be grateful. (Ibrahim 14: 37)

Allah answered His servant's prayer, and foiled Satan's strategem so that he was unable to sully the heart of that trusting believer. Thus, the rite of pelting with stones at Mina during the pilgrimage is to inform those who might not know that Allah's promise is real, that Satan's whisperings are meaningless and can affect only those whose hearts are devoid of the remembrance of Allah.

> Behold, he (Satan) has no power over those who have attained to faith and in their Lord place their trust: he has power only over those who are willing to follow him, and who thus ascribe to him a share in God's divinity. (al Nahal 16: 99-100)

An interesting point to note here is that the pelting at Mina is not mentioned by name in the Qur'an, but rather indicated in the verse exhorting the pilgrims to remember Allah during the appointed days of pilgrimage (at least two of which must be spent at Mina).

> And bear Allah in mind during the appointed days; but he who hurries away within two days shall incur no sin, and he who tarries longer shall incur no sin, provided that he is conscious of Allah. And know that unto Him you shall be gathered. (al Baqarah 2: 203)

It is as if the point of the entire exercise is the vocal remembrance of the Lord of all the Worlds, and the pelting a mere symbol. Indeed, the whole of pilgrimage is the continuous rumble of waves of humanity in constant remembrance of Allah. However, it is disturbing to note that the pelting with stones has recently become such a difficult rite to perform that only the most daring and adventurous of pilgrims are now capable of completing it, whereas the great majority including the old and infirm are made to suffer greatly because of it. Why! Because, in the opinion of the classical jurists, the rite may be performed only from when after the sun has passed its zenith until it actually sets. Thus, in a very limited period of time, a sea of surging humanity comes face to face with danger in a headlong rush to perform a symbolic rite.

Personally, I refuse to accept the opinion of the jurists in this particular matter because I know of no basis for it in either the Qur'an or the Sunnah. Thus, I have performed this rite at times in which both the crowds and the heat of the sun have been negligible.

Conditions have been ameliorated somewhat recently by the government of the Kingdom of Saudi Arabia which constructed a two tier platform for the rite, regulated the ways of approach and departure, and instructed the pilgrims that the rite may be performed at any time of day or night, thereby relieving untold suffering and easing the performance of an act of worship.

Yet there are some Muslims who would have us believe that pilgrimage is an incredibly complex and difficult matter. These are people who take pleasure in making ardous that which is essentially simple, and in giving currency to innovations which are devoid of any religious basis. Some of them even claim that there is a special *du'a* for each circumambulation of the Ka'bah, and a set of others for each passage from Safa to Marwah and back. Books have been written on the subject listing all the special *du'a*, none of which has any claim to legitimacy. These same people insist that the reward for running between Safa and Marwah on the ground floor of the colonnaded promenade erected between them by the Saudi Government is greater than that for running on the second floor. Likewise, the rite of pelting at Mina is supposed to be more meritorious when performed on the ground rather than from the platform! Perhaps they do not know that the Prophet of Allah, upon him be peace, performed the circumambulation while mounted on his camel, gesturing with a walking stick at the Black Stone from a distance.

In fact, pilgrimage is a loving and gentle form of worship consisting primarily of the standing at 'Arafah, the circumambulation of the Ka'bah, and a handful of lesser rites easily performed without the least difficulty or worry. Indeed, the religion of Islam demands the individual believer's sincerity, the maturity of his character, and the excellence of his relationship with his Lord, and of His worship. Concerning pilgrimage, it is written:

The pilgrimage shall take place in the months appointed for it. Whosoever undertakes the pilgrimage in those months shall, while on pilgrimage, abstain from lewd speech, from all wicked conduct, and from quarrelling; and whatever good you may do, Allah is aware of it. And make provision for yourselves. But, verily, the best of all provisions is God consciousness; remain, then, conscious of Me, O you who are endowed with insight! (al Baqarah 2: 197)

The journey to the holy places undoubtedly polishes the soul, cleanses the heart, and engenders love for Allah and His Prophet, and for all believers! It is then not surprising that the Prophet, upon him be peace, said,

Whoever undertakes a pilgrimage to this temple and abstains from lewd speech and wicked conduct, will shed his sins and become as pure as the day his mother gave birth to him or her.

It is an established fact that Makkah is the centre of the civilized world. Recently, Dr. Husain Kamal al Din, Professor of Engineering at Riyadh University, was able to prove through sophisticated mathematical calculations that Makkah is located at the physical centre of the inhabited continents, and that its position, as established by modern science, is a true commentary on the following verse of the Qur'an:

So We have revealed unto you a discourse in the Arabic tongue in order that you may warn the foremost of all cities and all who dwell around it — warn them of the Day of the Gathering, the coming of which is beyond all doubt. (al Shura 42: 7)

Around the glorious Ka'bah, then, extends a series of concentric circles of bowing and prostrating worshippers for whom the Sacred Mosque is their qiblah. Thus, on all latitudes and longitudes one can hear the call to prayer and witness the faithful in postures of submission to the One deserving of all Praise and Glory, the Lord of the Easts and the Wests, the Lord of all the Worlds.

During the pilgrimage season Makkah hosts delegations from every land on earth, to individuals united in their humanity, faith, and love for Allah and the first of all mosques, the foremost among mosques in the world. In Makkah, amidst a sea of surging faces, believing souls become acquainted with one another in harmonious reply to the call to pilgrimage, the call that has echoed since ancient times, and the call that has been strengthened and sharpened by Islam.

> Proclaim unto all people the pilgrimage: they will come to you on foot and on every kind of fast mount, coming from every far away point on earth so that they may experience much that is of benefit to them, and that they might remember the name of Allah on the days appointed . . . (al Hajj 22: 27-28)

And Allah's incoming delegations transform Makkah into a human society whose only interest is the remembrance of Allah and the calling out to Him by His blessed names.

In commerce various transactions prevail. In government offices the movement of files is the most apparent sign of life. But pilgrims in Makkah try to outbid one another in good deeds with prodigious shouts of 'Allah is the Greatest,' as if the earth were transformed with them into a far horizon teeming with devout angels.

Concerning the pilgrimage, Imam Nawawi wrote:

> It is preferable (*mustahabb*) that the pilgrim frequently call out 'Here I am, O Lord!, here I am . . .' This is preferable under all conditions, standing or sitting, walking or riding, reclining or descending, in a state of purity (*wudu'*) or in need of ablutions or a bath (during monthly courses), at the renewal of conditions and their changing either in time or space, like the coming of the day and night, at the time of

dawn, at the meeting of acquaintances, at the completion of prayers, and in every mosque . . .

If the pilgrim sees something which amazes him, he should say, 'Here I am! The only life is the life of the afterworld!' in emulation of the Prophet of Allah, upon him be peace.

The incident behind this was recorded by Imam Shafi'i on the authority of Mujahid who said, 'The Prophet of Allah, upon him be peace, was saying, "Here I am, O Lord, Here I am . . . !" throughout the rites of pilgrimage until one day the crowd pressed so hard upon him that those closest to him had to push people away from him. On realizing this situation, the Prophet was amazed, and said, "Here I am! The only life is the life of the afterworld."'[4]

It was the right of those tens of thousands of pilgrims to surround their Prophet, upon him be peace, as he fervently supplicated the Lord. He was, after all, their guide and leader. But Muhammad was not content to be crowded around by adoring followers. He was a leader of another sort. Indeed, his heart, attached as it was to the Almighty, and ever in anticipation of meeting Him, induced him to think of the afterlife, and wish that its morrow would draw closer.

At Safa, the Prophet, upon him be peace, was heard to say:

> «اَللَّهُ أَكْبَرُ اَللَّهُ أَكْبَرُ. اَللَّهُ أَكْبَرُ وَلِلَّهِ الْحَمْدُ. اَللَّهُ أَكْبَرُ
> عَلَى مَاهَدَانَا. وَالْحَمْدُ لِلَّهِ عَلَى مَا أَوْلَانَا. لَا إِلَهَ إِلَّا
> اللَّهُ وَحْدَهُ لَا شَرِيْكَ لَهُ، لَهُ الْمُلْكُ وَلَهُ الْحَمْدُ. يُحْيِيْ
> وَيُمِيْتُ، بِيَدِهِ الْخَيْرُ، وَهُوَ عَلَى كُلِّ شَيْءٍ قَدِيْرٌ. لَا إِلَهَ
> إِلَّا اللَّهُ، أَنْجَزَ وَعْدَهُ، وَنَصَرَ عَبْدَهُ، وَهَزَمَ الْأَحْزَابَ

---

[4] Commenting on this hadith, Ibn Jurayj said, 'I think this event occurred on the Day of 'Arafah.'

وَحْدَهُ. لَا إِلَهَ إِلَّا اللَّهُ، وَلَا نَعْبُدُ إِلَّا إِيَّاهُ مُخْلِصِينَ لَهُ

الدِّينَ، وَلَوْ كَرِهَ الْكَافِرُونَ. اَللَّهُمَّ إِنَّكَ قُلْتَ:

«أُدْعُونِيْ أَسْتَجِبْ لَكُمْ وَإِنَّكَ لَا تُخْلِفُ الْمِيْعَادَ. وَإِنِّيْ

أَسْأَلُكَ كَمَا هَدَيْتَنِيْ لِلإِسْلَامِ أَنْ لَا تَنْزِعَهُ مِنِّيْ حَتَّى

تَتَوَفَّانِيْ وَأَنَا مُسْلِمٌ...!».

Allah is the Greatest, Allah is the Greatest, Allah is the Greatest! To Allah is all praise! Allah is the Greatest for that to which He guided us, and to Allah is all praise for the favor He has rendered us. There is no god but Allah, He is One and has no partner, His is the domain and His is the praise. He gives life and takes it away. In His hand is all that is good, and He is powerful over everything. There is no god but Allah. He fulfilled His promise and gave victory to His servant, and defeated the confederates singlehandedly. There is no god but Allah! We worship none but Him, in all sincerity, though this be distasteful to the unbelievers! O Lord! You are the One who said, 'Call Me, and I will answer you' (al Mutmin 40: 60) and You never go back on Your promise, and so I entreat You, as You guided me to Islam, to never take it away from me; until finally You take my life and I depart this world as a Muslim.

God be praised! Is this not exactly the wish expressed by all the Prophets before him, upon all of whom be peace? After the Prophet Yusuf attained power, his prayer to Allah was that he die a believer:

O my Lord! You have bestowed upon me something of power, and have imparted to me some knowledge of the inner meaning of happenings. Originator of the heavens and the earth! You are near unto me in this world and in the life to come: let me die as one who has committed himself to You, and make me one with the righteous. (Yusuf 12: 101)

142

In the same way Muhammad prayed to his Lord during the Farewell Pilgrimage, having triumphed over idolatry, effaced the ways of the 'Days of Ignorance,' and established a state based on the Oneness of Allah.

What is really beautiful about his prayer is his mentioning, five years after the event, how Allah had given him victory over the confederates at the Battle of the Trench in Madinah; the victory that came as a bright, welcome dawn after a long night of adversity and fearful struggle.

This is Allah! The One who fulfilled His promise and singlehandedly defeated the confederates when no one else could blunt their cutting edge, or renting the fabric of their unity, or foiling their conspiracy. This is Allah! The only One worthy of thanks and of praise, the Fount of all God consciousness, and the Fount of all forgiveness.

Did the faith of Islam, or those who had attained to it, sit back and rest after these triumphs? By no means! The forces of disbelief will ever loathe the truth and those who stand for it. So the people of Islam will walk their path to the very end, regardless of how distasteful this may be to the disbelievers.

In citing the words and prayers used by the Prophet during the pilgrimage, I expected to record many *du'a*, and was therefore all the more surprised to discover the economy of words he, upon him be peace, actually used. Yet Muslims have since contrived different prayers and supplications for every circumambulation, and for every turn between Safa and Marwah; and for the Day of 'Arafah a virtual deluge of prayers! Nonetheless, I can appreciate the feelings behind this insistence. After all, it is not surprising that a pilgrim whose only desire is to please Allah should seek the assistance of any word which effectively translates his innermost emotions, or hold fast to any letter he feels may be the key to Allah's mercy.

One who seeks Allah's pleasure for himself and his family and stability in this world, should say Prophet Musa's *du'a*, upon him be peace:

O Lord! Surely I have need of whatever good You might send down upon me. (al Qasas 28: 24)

As for the *du'a* which the Prophet Muhammad, upon him be peace, never tired of repeating, during circumambulation, and between Safa and Marwah, it is this:

O our Lord! Grant us good in this world and good in the life to come, and keep us safe from suffering through the fire. (al Baqarah 2: 201)

And the hymn which echoes between the mountain summits and valleys is:

$$\text{«لَا إِلٰهَ إِلَّا اللّٰهُ وَحْدَهُ لَا شَرِيْكَ لَهُ، لَهُ الْمُلْكُ، وَلَهُ الْحَمْدُ، وَهُوَ عَلٰى كُلِّ شَيْءٍ قَدِيْرٌ».}$$

There is no god but Allah! He is One and has no partner. His is the dominion, and His is all praise, and He is Powerful over everything.

Thousands upon thousands call it out, and come together in doing so.

14

To Remember and Remind

From scorching heat, a person might seek refuge in the cool and comfort of an air-conditioned room. But more fortunate is he who can seek refuge in some cool, breezy resort where, regardless of the direction in which he might turn, there obtains an abiding freshness.

The relationship of a Muslim with his Lord, the Light of the Heavens and Earth, alternates between similar stages. Thus, a worshipper might live in a hermitage, secluded from the hubbub and temptations of society, in full communion with the Ever to be Praised, the Sublime, the Doer of what He Wills. Such a man is happy with his Lord, content to contemplate Him with his inward eye, far removed from the distorted and distorting heat of worldly life.

Or the Muslim might live in an environment of good, a place where Satan has acknowledged defeat and where truth abides in every place so that its expanses ring with the praise and glorification of Allah. There he can walk in the light of his faith and in that of his fellows who help him do good and remain conscious of Allah. The Sahabah, may Allah be pleased with them, enjoyed at the Prophet's side, upon him be peace, such an environment of abiding freshness in intimacy with Allah and the constant remembrance of His name.

The Prophet of Allah, as described by the Lord Himself, was 'a light giving Lamp' (al Ahzab 33: 46) whose beams stretched to every horizon and united all men in animated worship of the One True God. Thus, his light presided over an extensive world in which everything sang the praises of the Lord.

I have come to know something through my study of the life of the Last Prophet, upon him be peace, of the vast scope of the worship upon which his life was based. Yet I could not help but pause in wonder at the profundity of his worship represented in the hadith related by Ibn 'Abbas:

$$\text{«اَللّٰهُمَّ اكْتُبْ لِيْ بِهَا أَجْراً، وَحُطَّ عَنِّيْ بِهَا وِزْراً، وَاجْعَلْهَا لِيْ عِنْدَكَ ذُخْراً، وَتَقَبَّلْهَا مِنِّيْ كَمَا تَقَبَّلْتَهَا مِنْ عَبْدِكَ دَاوُدَ عَلَيْهِ الصَّلَاةُ وَالسَّلَامُ!!».}$$

A man went to the Prophet, upon him be the peace and blessings of Allah, and said, 'Last night, in a dream, I saw myself praying beneath a tree. When I prostrated myself, the tree prostrated too, and I heard it say: "O Lord! Write for me the recompense (of the prayer), delete because of it a sin, make of it a treasure for me, and accept it of me as You accepted it of the Prophet Dawud, upon him be peace."'

I later witnessed the Prophet of Allah, upon him be peace, prostrate and repeat the words of the tree as related by the man from his dream.

Now, as is apparent, the man who had the dream had been so completely absorbed the teachings of Islam that even in his sleep they gave fruit to his soul. But, more importantly, we learn that the heart of the Prophet, the Master, enveloped in the love of Allah, could be moved by anything spiritual so that it picked up the words of the *du'a*, ascribed to the tree, and so retained them that the Prophet could repeat them in his own prostration.

Indeed, the harmony of the Prophets with their Lord is one that reverberates at the slightest touch. Thus, when the Prophet Zakariyya discerned that a higher law had suspended the normal laws of cause and effect, and that divine beneficence had favored Maryam beyond all bounds, he inclined toward the Lord saying:

O my Lord! Bestow upon me too, out of Your grace, the gift of goodly offspring; for You, indeed, hear all prayer. (Al 'Imran 3: 38)

The ties which bind Muhammad, upon him be peace, to the Light of the Heavens and Earth are beyond all counting. His every effort was devoted to transforming his environment into one of worship, submission to Allah, remembrance of his name, and thanksgiving.

Imam Nasa'i related on the authority of Ya'qub ibn 'Asim that two of the Prophet's Companions heard him say, upon him be peace:

Whenever a believer says:

$$\text{لاَ إِلَهَ إِلاَّ اللهُ وَحْدَهُ لاَ شَرِيْكَ لَهُ، لَهُ اَلْمُلْكُ وَلَهُ الْحَمْدُ، وَهُوَ عَلَى كُلِّ شَيْءٍ قَدِيْرٌ.}$$

'There is no god but Allah. He is One and has no partner. His is the dominion and His is all praise; and He is Powerful over everything with the sincerity of his soul, the veracity of his heart, and the full power of utterance of his tongue, Allah parts the heavens asunder so that He may look down on that person on earth! And, of course, a person that Allah has especially looked upon deserves to receive what he or she asks for.

I will not mar this hadith's meaning by trying to explain the 'how' of what it contains. What it purports to say is that a believing heart, overflowing with sincerity and truth, will propel a declaration of belief from the believer's lips directly to the throne of the Almighty; and that thereafter the believer will never want for anything!

Such belief in Allah's Oneness as mentioned in this hadith and others comes out of a deep understanding of the significance of Allah's beautiful names and out of immersing oneself in their meanings. Certainly, a believer who learns how to praise Allah will never go away empty handed. I recollect the answer of one of Allah's gifted servants when asked about the best *du'a* for the Day of 'Arafah:

There is no god but Allah. He has no partner. His is the dominion and His is all praise; and He is powerful over everything.

'But that is praise', objected the questioner.

'Are you not familiar with what the poet said?' I asked. *'Need I mention my request, or will your modesty suffice me? Indeed, your most outstanding feature is your modesty. If today a man is lavish in his praise of you, his reward will come from the one his praise is directed to.'*

Tabrani relates that one of the *du'a* said by the Prophet, upon him be peace, on the Day of 'Arafah, is this:

«اَللَّهُمَّ إِنَّكَ تَرَى مَكَانِيْ، وَتَسْمَعُ كَلَامِيْ، وَتَعْلَمُ سِرِّيْ وَعَلَانِيَتِيْ، لَا يَخْفَى عَلَيْكَ شَيْءٌ مِنْ أَمْرِيْ.....أَنَا الْبَائِسُ الْفَقِيْرُ، الْمُسْتَغِيْثُ الْمُسْتَجِيْرُ، الْوَجِلُ الْمُشْفِقُ، الْمُقِرُّ الْمُعْتَرِفُ بِذَنْبِهِ، أَسْأَلُكَ مَسْأَلَةَ الْمِسْكِيْنِ، وَأَبْتَهِلُ إِلَيْكَ ابْتِهَالَ الْمُذْنِبِ الذَّلِيْلِ، وَأَدْعُوكَ دُعَاءَ الْخَائِفِ الضَّرِيْرِ.....مَنْ خَضَعَتْ لَكَ رَقَبَتُهُ، وَذَلَّ جَسَدُهُ وَرَغِمَ أَنْفُهُ....اَللَّهُمَّ لَا تَجْعَلْنِيْ بِدُعَائِكَ شَقِيًّا، وَكُنْ بِيْ رَؤُوفًا رَّحِيْمًا يَاخَيْرَ الْمَسْؤُوْلِيْنَ وَيَا خَيْرَ الْمُعْطِيْنَ».

O Lord, You see my position, and hear my petition, and know my inner and my outer condition! Nothing about me is hidden from You. I am a wretched beggar, a caller for help, fearful, anxious, and one who admits his sins. I supplicate

You as a miserable sinner, and I pray to You the prayer of a frightened blind man whose head is bowed, whose body is humbled and whose face is dusty O Lord! Do not make me one of the damned, but be Merciful and Compassionate towards me, O the Finest of those Petitioned and the Finest of Bestowers!

The link between praise and petition is also evident in this *du'a* of the Prophet, upon him be peace:

$$\text{«أَعُوذُ بِرِضَاكَ مِنْ سَخَطِكَ، وَأَعُوذُ بِمُعَافَاتِكَ مِنْ عُقُوبَتِكَ، وَأَعُوذُ بِكَ مِنْكَ، سُبْحَانَكَ لَا أُحْصِيْ ثَنَاءً عَلَيْكَ، أَنْتَ كَمَا أَثْنَيْتَ عَلَى نَفْسِكَ».}$$

I seek refuge in Your pleasure from Your wrath, and I seek refuge in Your favor from Your punishment, and I seek refuge in You from You, Glory be to You! I am incapable of counting Your praises. You are as You have praised Yourself!

And the same link is illustrated in this hadith:

The best *dhikr* is 'There is no god but Allah', and the best *du'a* is 'All praise to Allah.'

It is always worthwhile remembering that the mere moving of the lips means nothing unless what is being said is really an expression of inner reality. Regardless of how fine or how many the blessings, they fade into nothing in comparison with one's praise for the Giver of Blessings, and with one's appreciation for His favor.

Anas relates that the Prophet of Allah, upon him be peace, said:

Whenever Allah grants His favor to a servant and the servant says, "All praise to Allah" then he who receives becomes better than he who takes.'

149

And in another hadith:

> If the world and all that is in it were in the hand of a believer from my community, and he said 'All praise to Allah' then his praise of Allah would be better than all that he held in his hand.'

Commenting on that hadith, Imam Qurtubi (of Cordova) explained that the believer's receiving divine guidance to say words of praise is greater than the world and all it contains. For the reward for praise is eternal, whereas the bounty of this world is bound to perish. This is certainly a good explanation. Perhaps a more readily understandable explanation would be that the praise of Allah, blessed be His name, is sufficient as appreciation of His favor, and the means of securing it, regardless of how vast that favor may be.

Not everyone, obviously, is proficient in praising and thanking the Lord. Is it possible to give sincere praise to someone one does not know? Or thank someone one has no dealings with? The matter, as I explained earlier, is one which requires a deep understanding of the significance of the beautiful names of Allah. Only then can one appreciate the majesty of His being and attributes. Such an understanding requires a number of elements.

Among these is careful consideration of the Qur'an in which the Almighty Lord speaks of Himself and shows His signs. An ordinary person, if he notices the coming of day, and its passing into night at all, will do so without much reflection. But the Qur'an seeks to stir his consciousness by asking who has caused all this to happen.

> He is the One who causes the dawn to break; and He has made the night to be a source of stillness, and the sun and the moon to run their appointed courses; all this is laid down by the will of the Almighty, the All knowing. (al An'am 6: 96)

One often sees, without really noticing, prodigious expanses of fields and gardens in which the solid earth splits open to push up every variety of grain and fruit. Who caused this wondrous process? Who filled this greenery with sugar, foodstuffs and perfume?

> And He it is who has caused waters to come down from the sky; and by this means have We brought forth all living growth, and out of this have We brought forth verdure. Out of this do We bring forth close growing grain; and out of the spathe of the palm tree, dates in thick clusters; and gardens of vines and the olive tree, and the pomegranate: all so alike, and yet so different!. (al An'am 6: 99)

In this way, after clearly directing the attention of His servant to such evidences, the Master subtly wins him over; the Lord of all the Worlds subtly wakes the many from their negligent slumber:

> Behold their fruit when it comes to fruition and ripens! Verily, in all this there are messages indeed for people who will believe! (al An'am 6: 99)

The contemplation of nature is most certainly a wide doorway, opening directly upon knowledge of the beautiful names of Allah and their meanings and relation to Him.

Beside the contemplation of nature comes the contemplation of the condition of individuals and societies, the study of history, past and present; how our Lord gives and how He takes away!

The distance is not great between Pharaoh's indignant statement:

> I did not know that you could have any deity other than myself. (al Qasas 28: 38)

and his last words before the angry waves swallowed him up:

> I have come to believe that there is no deity save Him in whom the children of Israel believe. (Yunus 10: 90)

But we are ever victims of the present hour, as if we had been given no means to study the ways of Allah with individuals or groups. How many societies attained the highest peak of accomplishment and civilization, only to stumble into oblivion not long after?

> Thus We requited them for their having denied the truth. But do We ever requite (thus) any but the utterly ingrate? (Saba' 34: 17)

The Qur'an is full of every kind of example whose purpose is to bring people closer to knowledge of their Lord, to enable them to contemplate and heed Him, and to plant within them the seeds of desire and awe. The Prophet, upon him be peace, once said and this shows how desire and awe are stressed simultaneously —

> If the believer came to know of the kind of punishment, Allah has prepared, his thought would never turn toward the attractions of Paradise. And if the disbeliever came to know of the mercy of Allah, then never would anyone despair of attaining it!

It is essential that all theoretical knowledge of the universe, of its laws, and of its inhabitants, science or history, be transformed into experience and action. Otherwise it becomes like an electric current prevented by some non-conducting material, so that it is incapable of lighting a light or powering a machine.

Knowledge must be actualized. Let me here affirm that no man knew his Lord nor realized that knowledge more fully or greatly than Muhammad ibn 'Abdullah, so entirely had every atom of his physical existence been transformed into the power of surrender to Him. His whole character and personality were composed of the Qur'an so that he internalized its meanings and moved entirely within its orbit. For this reason he was ever drawn toward the signs of Allah through the guidance of revelation and the vastness of his own spirituality. For this reason, too, he drew whoever he came into contact with to the same elevated level of purity, and raised him into a spiritual master, a custodian of the authority of Allah. That is why his Companions were the most certain of all people in faith, and the purest in nature.

It is hard to believe that anyone could ever find a way that leads to Allah, if he knows nothing about Muhammad, upon him be peace.

The most prominent aspect of the life of this Prophet, upon him be peace, is that his love for Allah, his exaltation of Allah, and his self-annihilation in Allah were transmitted to those around him. Thus, it was as if they were engaged in a race to praise Allah and to extol Him. Consider this hadith:

Imam Ahmad related on the authority of 'Abd Allah ibn 'Umar that a servant from among the true servants of Allah said:

$$\text{وَيَارَبِّ لَكَ الْحَمْدُ كَمَا يَنْبَغِيْ لِجَلَالِ وَجْهِكَ،}$$

$$\text{وَلِعَظِيْمِ سُلْطَانِكَ......}$$

'O Lord! Praise to You as is befitting of the majesty of Your countenance and the magnificence of Your authority!'

This so puzzled the man's two guardian angels that they did not know how to write it down, and they flew up into the heavens where they said, 'O Lord! Your servant has said something today which we know not how to record!' The Lord replied, and He knows best what His servant said, 'What did My servant say?'

They replied, 'He said, "O Lord! Praise to You as is befitting of the majesty of Your countenance and the magnificence of Your authority!"'

So Allah said to them, 'Write it as My servant has said it; and when he meets Me, I will recompense him for it.'

153

Manifestly, this servant had been on a spiritual journey which took him to horizons known only to Allah, and gathered there such signs and wisdom as charged his heart, and drowned his senses, and so overcame his inner and outer being that he could see only to greet his Lord with those words. And the two angels, realizing that what he had said was beyond the scope of the instructions they had concerning the entry of rewards for words spoken in the book of deeds, did as they were told.

> Abu Ayyub related that a man said, in the presence of the Prophet of Allah, upon him be peace, 'Praise to Allah, praise that is abundant, good and blessed!'
>
> When the Prophet asked the man where he had learned these words, the man remained silent, thinking that in some way he had offended the Prophet. So the Prophet of Allah, upon him be peace, said, 'Whose words are they? For, indeed, he has said only what is correct!'
>
> At that, the man replied, 'I said them, O Prophet of Allah, and I only meant well by them.'
>
> The Prophet, upon him be peace, said, 'By the one who holds my life in His hand! I saw thirteen different angels vying with one another for the privilege of bringing your words to the attention of the Almighty!'

Anas ibn Malik related that,

> Ubayy ibn Ka'b said: 'I will go to the mosque and pray, and then praise Allah with praises never used before by anyone!' When Ubayy had finished his prayer and was sitting, about to begin his praise, he heard a voice behind him saying, 'O Lord, Yours is all praise in its entirety. Yours is all dominion in its entirety, and in Your hand is all good in its entirety. Unto You returns all authority in its entirety, what is manifest of it and what is secret. Praise be unto You! You are

Powerful over everything. Forgive me what has passed of my sins, and prevent me from sinning the rest of my life. Bless me with deeds of purity which will ensure for me Your pleasure, and accept my repentance.'

Immediately, Ubayy went to the Prophet of Allah, upon him be peace, and told him what had happened. The Prophet said, 'That was the Angel of the Lord, Jibril, upon whom be peace!'

Nor is there anything extraordinary about an angel descending with the words of a *du'a* for the express purpose of transmitting them to a heart which trembles with the desire to give praise to Allah in a manner in which He has never been praised before. Indeed, the descent of angels at times when the Sahabah were reciting the Qur'an is mentioned in numerous hadith.

Rather, one is led to ask who impelled the Sahabah to apply themselves so intensely in the way of Allah's Unity and worship that their tongues flowed with springs of wisdom and words of great purity in His praise and glorification? It was the Prophet Muhammad, upon him be peace! Who else could have been responsible for such ardor? This was the man, the ever worshipping, ever prostrating, ever remembering, ever thanksgiving, who was inspired to praise and glorify the Lord with every movement and breath. Truly, this was the man who transformed the earth into an arena for competition with the heavenly hosts in remembrance and thanksgiving.

Nu'man ibn Bashir related that the Prophet of Allah, upon him be peace, said,

Whatever you mention in the way of exalting Allah, be it praise, glorification, or recitation of the creed of Islam (there is no god but Allah), will circle around the throne of the Almighty and buzz like the buzzing of bees with the name of the one who mentioned it. Would any one of you like to be mentioned in this manner?

'Abd Allah ibn Mas'ud said:

Whenever I relate a hadith to you, I verify its meaning with a verse from the Book of Allah. Whenever a believer says "Glory be to Allah, and praise to Allah, and there is no god except Allah; Allah is the Greatest and blessed is Allah!," an angel grasps his words, places them safely under his wing, and soars heavenward with them. Along the way, all the angels that he passes ask forgiveness for that believer until, finally, the words are offered in greeting to the All Merciful.

Then 'Abd Allah recited the following verse of the Qur'an:

Unto Him ascend all good words, and the righteous deed does He exalt. (al Fatir 35: 10)

They say that one who himself does not possess something cannot possibly give that something to another. To complete the meaning of this saying, I might add that one who gives a great deal must himself possess a great deal more! Dried up streams will only begin to flow following a heavy downpour that continues day and night.

The truth is that our pious predecessors, those who took their lessons directly from the Prophet, and each successive generation of the righteous who follow in their footsteps to the end of time, both groups were, are or will be, influenced by the personality of Muhammad, upon him be peace, take their inner light from his spirituality, and draw their strength from the stability of his faith.

Undoubtedly, his companionship during his lifetime, or the companionship of his intellectual and moral legacies after his death could, and still can, work miracles. It is in proportion to the amount of the charge taken from the source that the powers of spirit or intellect may develop. Obviously, the foundation of those powers is the magnitude of the source.

Between the sun and the earth are one hundred and fifty million kilometers. This is in regard of distance. We have no idea, in regard of time, when the sun first shone. Nonetheless, neither the remoteness of space nor of time has appreciably altered the sun's ability to illuminate, to ripen, or to support life on this planet. So too, the effect of Muhammad, upon him be peace, on early and later generations; the effect of his worship and leadership, the effect of his example and message, regardless of how much time has passed, or distance.

There is a need to explain further the way of remembrance and reminding in the Last Prophet's mission, upon him be peace. The first principle is intellectual integrity. Thus, the words and phrases which Islam encourages its followers to repeat are all based on rationally sound propositions. For example, the phrases 'There is no god but Allah' or 'Glory be to Allah' or 'Exalted be Allah;' the meaning of each of these phrases is essentially the affirmation of the truth of the most important principles of belief. Consider the words of Allah:

> Never did Allah take unto Himself any offspring, nor has there ever been any deity side by side with Him; for, had there been any, lo! each deity would surely have stood apart from the others in whatever it had created, and they would surely have tried to overcome one another! Limitless in His glory is Allah, far above anything that man may devise by way of definition, knowing all that is beyond the reach of a created being's perception as well as all that can be witnessed by a creature's senses or mind and, hence, sublimely exalted is He above anything to which they may ascribe a share in His divinity. (al Mu'minin 23: 91-92)

Allah has no mother, and no father, and no son, and no daughter. He is One. Besides Him there is the slave who is subservient to His authority. Should the Master will, the favor of His slave's existence could be withdrawn, so that he perishes and fades.

Indeed, everything other than Allah is merely a speck in a vast universe which is sustained by the will of Allah, after He willed it into being in the first instance. Like a light, it could go out at the figurative flick of a switch!

Nothing, no one, shares in His divinity; there is no power and no strength save in Allah. His alone is grace, dominion and majesty. And Muhammad, upon him be peace, was the most outspoken of all men in proclaiming these truths. Through his words and deeds he was able to remove any number of the crude superstitions with which these truths had become contaminated, thus delivering multitudes that had gone astray.

No one in the history of humankind ever undertook the labor that he undertook, or achieved the success that he achieved. Nor do I know of anyone who more enraged, or obstructed the wrongdoing of, the devils and the recalcitrant from among men and jinn than the Prophet Muhammad, upon him be peace. Thus was the truth established over falsehood; and thus the right way became distinct from the way of error.

The Prophet who stood so long in nightly prayer, upon him be peace, gatheredan army of believers whose resounding cry of 'Allah is the Greatest' would all but split asunder the clouds. This was the cry that Allah is One, and that all creatures including the first among them, Muhammad, are His slaves, slaves to the One whose blessings flow over them, and whose wisdom orders their lives.

If religion can be said to be a good heart, then even before; that it is a healthy mind, sound reflection, and correct knowledge.

> Allah Himself proffers evidence and so do the angels and all who are endowed with knowledge that there is no deity save Him, the Upholder of Equity; there is no deity save Him. The Almighty, the Truly Wise. (Al 'Imran 3: 18)

We Muslims never tire of repeating that statement because the world is full of people who say that God has a mother, or a father, or that He is the union of three divine persons: Father, Son and Holy

Spirit. Now this is a statement which is totally devoid of truth. The source of its currency could only have been infirm minds with fantastic ideas bordering on the absurd! Certainly no Prophet before or after ever said such a thing; and no one who respects his intellect would ever uphold it!

The People of the Book, and I mean the Christians in particular, cannot tolerate the Islamic creed of Allah's Unity. In the past they have crusaded against it, and they continue to do so today. Nevertheless, we shall hold fast to it, and meet our Lord with it.

Imam Ahmad related on the authority of Shaddad ibn Aws, whose narration was verified by Ubadah ibn Samit, who said,

> Once we were with the Prophet, upon him be peace and blessings, when he said, 'Are there any strangers among us?,' meaning from the People of the Book. We said, 'No, O Prophet of Allah.' Then he ordered that the door be closed and said, 'Raise your hands and say "There is no god but Allah"' as if taking a pledge of our allegiance. When we had held our hands up for some time he said, 'All praise to Allah! O Lord, verily have You sent me with this creed, and charged me with it, and promised me by means of it Your paradise, and You never go back on a promise!' Then he said, 'Rejoice, for Allah has forgiven your sins!'

Yet no matter how sound or keen our intellects, there is no substitute for purity of heart and soul. Even Satan (Iblis) knew that Allah is One. But he refused to be obedient, refused to be humble and deny himself, refused to suppress his eruptions of hatred and malice for others, refused to be a true slave to Allah.

The vast moral framework erected by the Last of the Prophets, upon him be peace, can be supported only by those whose hearts are unblemished. That is why the Prophet, upon him be peace, pointed to his heart and said,

Heedfulness is here! Heedfulness is here! Heedfulness is here!

After the Qur'an has explained these intellectual truths, it explains spiritual and moral truths and the conduct necessary to their maintenance.

> Verily your Lord is Allah, who has created the heavens and the earth in six eons, and is established on the throne of His Almightiness. He covers the day with night in swift pursuit, with the sun and the moon and the stars, subservient to His command: Oh, verily, His is all creation and all command. Hallowed is Allah, the Lord of all the Worlds! Call unto your Lord humbly, and the secrecy of your hearts. Verily, He loves not those who transgress the bounds of what is right. Hence, do not spread corruption on earth after it has been so well ordered. And call unto Him with fear and longing: Verily, Allah's grace is near unto the doers of good! (al A'raf 7: 54-56)

At another place in the same surah, Allah says:

> And bethink yourself of your Lord humbly and with awe, and without raising your voice, at morn and at evening; and do not allow yourself to be heedless. (al A'raf 7: 205)

The kind of remembrance which is sought here is the movement of the heart, not the movement of the tongue; a movement of the heart which points one in this or that direction, which animates him or slows him down. It is related that the mother of Anas said,

> 'O Prophet of Allah! Give me some good advice,' to which he, upon him be peace, replied, 'Emigrate from sin, for assuredly that is the best kind of emigration! Be diligent in the performance of the obligatory duties, for assuredly that is the best kind of jihad! And remember Allah often, for assuredly you cannot meet Allah with anything better than His remembrance!'

The kind of *dhikr* recommended in this hadith is not the same as that commonly known as remembrance. It is, rather, one's source of contentment and stability in the face of worldly adversities and hardships. In our own contemporary civilization, there are many educated people, each with his own set of intelligent acquaintances. Yet, in spite of all our sophistication, nervous disorders and depression are common ailments. For the reason that the hearts of men are devoid of Allah. Hearts which never remember Allah, or incline His way, are not likely to establish for their possessors even the frailest sort of relationship with Him. And, after all, how can they remember someone they do not even know? Indeed, for the most part, modern civilization is completely disconnected from Allah.

Yet man, regardless of how strong he may be, is essentially weak; and regardless of how knowledgeable he may be, is essentially inadequate. Indeed, man's need for his Lord is no less than that of a child for its parent.

For the believer, remembrance of Allah at times of crisis and difficulty provides solace and hope.

> Those who believe, and whose hearts find their rest in the remembrance of Allah — for, verily, in the remembrance of Allah men's hearts do find their rest — they who attain to faith and do righteous deeds are destined for happiness (in this world) and the most beauteous of all goals [in the life to come]. (al Ra'd 13: 28-9)

Muhammad, upon him be peace, was the most trusting of all people, and the closest, in his relationship to Allah. In the earliest days of his mission, he was told:

> And remember your Lord's name, and devote yourself unto Him with utter devotion. The Lord of the East and the West is He; there is no deity save Him: hence, take Him as your Guardian. (al Muzammil 73: 8-9)

And from that day onward he put all his trust in Allah, and faced the forces of disbelief and idolatry steadfastly, and without wincing. He taught mankind to be confident of Allah's compassion for them, and of His mercy toward them. Why, he asked, when Allah is more compassionate and merciful to them than a mother is to the child she feeds at her breast, why should people stray, and seek to flee from Him?

The single most important element in a conscience which abhors sin and shields its possessor from deviation is the remembrance of Allah. There are people who literally strain their vocal cords shouting the name of Allah, but I would not wish to say that those are the ones who truly remember Allah. I mean, rather, those who are ever conscious that Allah is watching over them:

> We shall most certainly reveal them Our knowledge of their doings: for never have We been absent [from them]. (al A'raf 7: 7)

One who remembers in this way will, when faced with an opportunity to do wrong, abstain; and if Satan makes the abominable appear attractive to him, he will uncover the deception and refuse to follow him, remember the majesty of his Lord, His commandments and His prohibitions, and then, remain upright. Such a man is the noble and chaste rememberer referred to in the Qur'anic verse:

> But unto him who shall have stood in fear of his Lord's presence, and held back his inner self from base desires, paradise will truly be the goal. (al Nazi'at 79: 40-41)

How numerous the tongues that move with the name of Allah! But how meager the benefit! And how rare the hearts that become genuinely humble at the mention of Allah! Yet how desperate the need of the world for those rare hearts!

Undoubtedly, the ruin of religion comes about when it digresses into empty words and forms. And the mission of religion will not have been accomplished until the day it creates in all men living conscience, pure mind and hearts that aim in awe at countenancing the divine. That is what true *dhikr* is!

One of the influences of this kind of *dhikr* is that it curbs man's appetite for wealth. Thus, those who remember Allah are never obsessed by greed for more and more, and are certainly never demeaned by greedy or covetous constitutions. Rather, they earn their money honestly, and spend it on their legitimate needs without ever thinking to hoard or accumulate it. Thus nothing but good awaits them in money matters. It would seem that all religious impostors inevitably get caught up in the snare of wealth, in amassing or accumulating it. Often, for the sake of it, they cooperate with, or turn a blind eye toward, corrupt rulers and officials; thus paving the way for atheistic philosophies to come in and rule where the reputation of religion, and those who speak in its name, have been tarnished.

By contrast the Prophet Muhammad, upon him be peace, distributed among the people every bit of wealth which came his way. Indeed, when he departed this world, there was nothing to be distributed among his heirs! In addition, he brought up an entire generation of people who preferred the countenance of the Lord to the riches of the world:

> Who give food, however great be their own want of it, unto the needy, and the orphan, and the captive, [saying in their hearts] We feed you for the sake of Allah alone. We desire no recompense from you, nor thanks. (al Dahr 76: 8-9)

It is interesting to note that the ten from among the Companions who received good tidings of their acceptance in Paradise were people of considerable wealth who had relinquished it for the sake of Allah.

This is not to say that salvation lies in renouncing one's wealth and family. On the contrary, salvation lies in one's having great wealth and a large family, and then while fulfilling all responsibilities to them, not allowing them to distract one from remembrance of the Lord.

O you who have attained to faith! Let not your worldly goods or your children make you oblivious to the remembrance of Allah: for if any behave thus, it is they, they who are the losers! And spend on others out of what We have provided for you as sustenance, ere there comes a time when death approaches any one of you, and then says, 'O my Lord! If only You would grant me a delay for a short while, so that I could give in charity and be among the righteous! (al Munafiqun 63: 9-10)

The remembrance of Allah influences character and pesonality in many ways. But this is not the place to attempt to list them all. Suffice it to say that remembrance of the Almighty elevates one's standing with Him, restrains one from tyranny, and moves one to regard all things in their proper perspective.

Who taught mankind to know their Lord, and reminded them of their duties toward Him, and put to rest the baseless rumors concerning belief in religion, and clarified that there is no god save Allah? Of course, Muhammad, upon him be peace. But how did he achieve success in leading successive generations along the straight path?

When he first began to preach the new religion in Makkah, the overwhelming majority of people were furious with him:

And yet, they say: 'O you unto whom this reminder has (allegedly) been bestowed from on high: verily, you are mad!' (al Hijr 15: 6)

But he marched on toward his goal, battling the forces of obsessive pride and egotism, until finally, through Allah's deliverance, he established the state of the truth. Throughout this time, the Qur'an was his morality. The study of its meanings was the core of his thought and the current of his consciousness; its teachings, its commandments, and its prohibitions were the substance of his behavior and the basis of all his relations with people. But the recitation of the Qur'an was the felicity of his soul!

In a hadith it is related:

> Never has Allah allowed to anyone what He allows to a Prophet who recites the Qur'an melodiously.

In this way the revelation emanating from Allah is applied on earth in legal and moral codes, and then returns to heaven in the notes of a melodious recitation.

It will not be out of place here to mention a story of the impact that the Qur'an had on the soul of a man while he was still an idolater.

Jubayr ibn Mut'im related that his father traveled to Madinah as a negotiator for the Quraysh entrusted with the mission of ransoming captives taken at the Battle of Badr. Obviously, his father was one of the most important leaders of the Quraysh. No less important was the purpose of the journey: freeing upwards of seventy Qurayshi notables whose arrogance had made them captives of the Muslims.

It so happened that the man overheard the Prophet of Allah as he recited from the Qur'an in prayer. Later, he told his son, 'Never had I heard a more beautiful voice or recitation than his.' Thus the man stood in rapt attention, listening to the verses coming from within the mosque. Mut'im said to his son, 'When he reached these verses

—

> Or have they themselves been created without any thing? Or were they, perchance, their own creators? And have they created the heavens and the earth? Nay, but they have no certainty of anything. (al Tur 52: 35-36)

— my heart nearly flew away!'

And his overhearing the recitation of these verses became the reason for his acceptance of Islam.

Let us reflect on this a little. The surah from which these verses are taken was revealed in the Makkan period of the Prophet's mission and must have been recited hundreds of times there. How was it possible, then, that the envoy of the Quraysh could have heard these verses for the first time in Madinah several years after the emigration from Makkah? One possibility is that he never heard them because of the practice of the idolaters in Makkah of raising as noisy a commotion as possible whenever the Muslims gathered to read and study the Qur'an. Another possibility is that he had heard it before, but that because of prejudice and pride he was blinded to the truth. Then, after the sobering defeat suffered by the Quraysh he may have returned to his senses, and begun to listen humbly and with attention to what he heard.

I have myself considered the verses which so moved and delighted this man's heart, and found that they renewed within me the perception of the wisdom which they contain. They are brief, but they have a sharp, penetrating solemnity which, so much like a fine and delicate key to the lock of some immense treasure, throw the heart open to the verses' meaning, sweeping in with the recitation like a gust of wind.

The word 'or' is used as a rhetorical device some fifteen times in these verses. According to scholars of Arabic rhetoric, the article 'am' (or) is often used for expostulation when it is followed by a question of a rhetorical, reproaching or marveling nature. Consider, as we ponder these verses, how they act to rid the human soul of its heedlessness, and force it to pay attention to the truth.

> Remind, then, [O Prophet, all men] for, by the grace of your Lord, you are neither a soothsayer nor a madman. Or do they say [he is but] a poet, let us await what time will do to him? Say: 'Wait hopefully: behold, I too shall wait hopefully with you!' Is it their minds that bid them [to take] this [atti-

tude] or are they simply people filled with overweening arrogance? Or do they say 'He himself has composed this message?' Nay, but they are not willing to believe! But then, [if they deem it the work of a mere mortal] let them produce another discourse like it if what they say be true! Or have they themselves been created without any thing? Or were they, perchance, their own creators? And have they created the heavens and the earth? Nay, but they have no certainty of anything. Are your Lord's treasures with them? Or are they in charge of destiny? Or have they a ladder by which they could listen [to what is beyond the reach of human perception]? Let, then, any of them who has listened produce a manifest proof [of his knowledge]! Or, [if you believe in Allah, how can you believe that] He has [chosen to have] daughters, whereas you your selves would have [only] sons? Or is it that you ask of them a reward, so that they would be burdened with debt [if they should pay it to you]? Or [do they think] that the hidden reality [of all that exists] is almost within their grasp, so that they can write it down? Or do they want to entrap you in contradictions? But they who are bent on denying the truth it is they who are truly entrapped! Have they, then, any god other than Allah? Utterly remote is Allah, in His limitless glory, from anything to which men may ascribe a share in His divinity! (al Tur 52: 29-43)

These are the Qur'anic verses which produced such a powerful effect on the heart of an idolater.

It is related that the *khalifah*, 'Umar ibn al Khattab, was on his rounds of the city one night when he passed the house of a believer who was standing in prayer and reciting from the Qur'an. The *khalifah* halted outside and listened until the man recited the following verse:

Verily, the suffering decreed by your Lord [for the sinners] will indeed come to pass. (al Tur 52: 7)

He then exclaimed:

'By the Lord of the Ka'bah, that is true!'

Then, he dismounted and leaned against a wall for support as he was stricken with awe, until he was composed enough to return to his house where he remained for a full month receiving visitors who asked after his health and speculated among themselves as to the cause of his infirmity.

Such was 'Umar, the Commander of the Faithful, whose breast was filled to overflowing with dread of the Almighty, riding through the city's quarters at night in unobserved inspection of his subjects. The great man who carried the burden of the affairs of the whole ummah and was kept awake by his own answerability for it to the point where it might suddenly prove too much, was now beset by an illness in the form of fear born of awe and reverence for the Almighty.

Umar, if it be the will of Allah, will certainly receive a handsome reward in the life to come for all that he did in the service of Islam and the Muslims. Yet, the heart of a sensitive believer knows no peace until it can, at last, meet its Lord.

The reason for my mentioning this story here is that I am so angered by the lack of refinement of the audiences who crowd round long-winded reciters of the Qur'an, who shout out or posture gracelessly, without understanding anything of what they hear. Surely such gatherings are a travesty of what should be. Yet how often, alas, do Muslims abuse the Book of Allah!

The Qur'anic verses which caused a perceptive man's heart to soar in awe, delivering him from idolatry to faith in Allah, began with a single lucid statement:

Remind, then, [O Prophet, all men] for, by the grace of your Lord, you are neither a soothsayer, nor a madman. (al Tur 52: 29)

The reminding referred to here is the conception and execution of a plan for a new way of life based on divine revelation and guidance.

Remembrance, here, is thus a sort of transaction with Allah, one in which both zeal and value are, if the expression be admissible, 'exchanged' — and to Allah belong the sublimest degrees of all attributes. This well-known *hadith qudsi* clarifies the meaning:

> Allah says, 'I am as My servant imagines Me to be, and I am always with him. Thus, if he remembers Me in private, I remember him in private. And if he remembers Me in company, I will remember him in better company. If he advances an inch toward Me, I will advance a foot toward him. If he advances a foot toward Me, I will advance a yard toward him. And if he advances toward Me at a walk, I will advance toward him at a run.

The version related by Imam Ahmad contains the following words:

> And Allah is the swiftest to grant forgiveness.

The kind of *dhikr* being discussed is a person's resolute turning to Allah, and Allah's acceptance of the same where, obviously, Allah's approach is more sublime, and purer.

On this matter, the Prophet, upon him be peace, said a number of enlightening things from which we may assuredly benefit:

> Whoever says, 'There is no god but Allah', with all sincerity, will enter Paradise.

When the Prophet, upon him be peace, was asked to explain what he meant by 'sincerity'; he replied:

> One's refraining from all that Allah has prohibited.

In another hadith, he, upon him be peace, said:

There are two phrases which, in spite of their lightness on the tongue, are heavy in the measure, and well beloved by the All Merciful:

$$\text{«سُبْحَانَ اللهِ وَبِحَمْدِهِ،}$$

'Glory be to Allah and in His praise'

and

$$\text{سُبْحَانَ اللهِ الْعَظِيْمِ.»}$$

'Glory be to Allah, the Almighty'.

In a similar vein, the Prophet of Allah, upon him be peace, said:

Cleanliness is half of faith. The words 'All praise to Allah' fill the scales, and the words, 'Glory to Allah and All praise to Allah' fill all that is between heaven and earth. Prayer is light (*nur*), charity is proof, patience is luminance, and the Qur'an is a witness either for or against you. Everyone who faces the new day is either a seller of his soul, an emancipator of it, or its devastator.

Once a bedouin of the desert said to the Prophet, upon him be peace,

'O Prophet of Allah! I have tried to memorize something of the Qur'an, but am unable to retain anything. Teach me something which will do just as well!' The Prophet, upon him be peace, replied: 'Say, "Glory be to Allah, All praise to Allah, there is no god but Allah, and Allah is the Greatest."' The bedouin then said: 'O Prophet of Allah! That is for my Lord. What is for me?' The Prophet answered: 'Say "O Lord, forgive me, have mercy on me, grant me ease, and keep me provided for."' When the bedouin had gone on his way, the Prophet, upon him be peace, said: 'The bedouin has left with both hands full of good.'

The hadiths which have been related and preserved on this subject are many. Indeed, one who writes on the subject of the Prophet's character might be led to believe, by the vastness of the material available on the subject, that the entire Sunnah (way) of the Prophet was devoted to character. While one who writes on jihad, or *dhikr*, might be led to believe that the entire Sunnah was devoted to jihad or *dhikr*.

The greatness of the Prophet is something which can literally exhaust the curious. Glory be to the One who sent him as a Mercy for all the Worlds!

O Lord! Praise be to You in all fullness unto all eternity! Praise be to You unto the ends of Your knowledge! Praise be to You unto the ends of Your will! [And the knowledge and will of Allah are without end!] And praise be to You in which the only reward of the one who voices it is Your pleasure!

15

THE PROPHET OF PEACE
AND THE PROPHET OF WAR

No one who respects his own honesty could possibly accuse Muhammad, upon him be peace, of seeking through his mission, wealth, position or any of the worldly pleasures.

Those who are acquainted with his life story know that he was the mightiest in declaring the teaching of Allah's unity and divine majesty, the most outspoken in denying that the Almighty had partners in divinity or mediators, the most eager of all to carry out His orders, show respect for His revelation, and to prevent his human desires from interfering in what He had legislated.

The Prophet, upon him be peace, was deeply grieved and hurt by the opposition shown to him by the ignorant, distressed and made anxious by their persistent blindness. But Allah made it clear to him that he was charged with no more than delivering the divine message:

We did not reveal the Qur'an to you from on high to make you unhappy, but only as a reminder to all who stand in awe [of Allah]. (Ta Ha 20: 2)

The Almighty gave him to understand that people could not be brought to the straight path by force, and that no amount of zeal or sincerity could induce people to believe:

And [thus it is] had your Lord so willed, all those who live on earth would surely have attained faith, all of them. Do you think, then, that you could compel people to believe?. (Yunus 10: 99)

Nevertheless, the followers of the other religions sensed danger in the new call, and felt that their allowing the Prophet to preach his message unopposed would amount to their losing their following. For indeed (as they may rightly have noted) there is a natural affinity of the human soul for Islam: it is completely acceptable to reason, and the heart is drawn to it without constraint.

For these reasons, the enemies of Islam determined very early on to prevent its gaining currency by whatever means necessary. Had those included a point for point debate on the relative merits of each religion, Islam would gladly have welcomed the chance to explain itself, secure in the knowledge of the ultimate result. But no. The matter went the way of the politics of arrogance and provocation; the only kind of politics in which the powerful seem to be proficient.

But they who denied the truth spoke thus unto their prophets: 'We shall most certainly expel you from our land, unless you return forthwith to our ways'. (Ibrahim 14: 13)

These were the politics which left the Prophet, for all his patience, no alternative but to stand up in defense of his mission and of those oppressed souls who were forced to suffer along with him because they dared to believe.

Suppose that you were walking outside at night with a torch in your hand to light your, or someone else's, way. If there were others who found it distasteful to follow you, or walk by your light, they would certainly be welcome to take any direction they wished, avoiding the pitfalls and obstacles as best they could.

Means of insight have now come unto you from your Lord. Whoever, therefore, chooses to see, does so for his own good; and whoever chooses to remain blind, does so to his own detriment. (al An'am 6: 104)

174

But what is one to do if those who prefer to remain in the dark try to break your torch and put out its light? Do you not have right to defend the light that guides you and so many others? This was all that Muhammad, upon him be peace, did:

> Who could be more wicked than one who invents a lie about Allah; seeing that he is but being called to Islam? But Allah does not bestow His guidance upon evil doing folk. They aim to extinguish Allah's light with their utterances; but Allah has willed to spread His light in all its fullness, however hateful this may be to all who deny the truth. He it is who has sent forth His Prophet with the task of spreading guidance and the religion of truth, to the end that He makes it prevail over all false religion, however hateful this may be to those who ascribe divinity to aught but Allah. (al Saff 61: 7-9)

Indeed, those who advocate the politics of torch breaking are the most virulent of all people in their loathing of Muhammad, upon him be peace, and in the abhorrence of the message he brought to mankind. These are the people who know in their hearts that that light is their greatest enemy because it reveals their deception. If intellectual freedom is allowed, then, in the light of it, the doctrine of the trinity must be rejected — even if cunningly explained that a triangle is made from one line.

Consider the mission of Muhammad, upon him be peace. Can we see in it even the faintest trace of personal gratification or worldly glorification? Can we see in the lifetime of any human being anything to match the fervor of his teachings with regard to Allah, His Oneness, and the need to lose one's self in obtaining His pleasure? Next, consider the battles he fought. Did he rely upon his own strength, or trust in the power and resources of Allah? Did he ever seek anything more or other than that the name of Allah be exalted? Did he ever say, 'Woe to the vanquished' or act in such a way as to suggest it? Did he not rather establish religious freedom as the right of one and all, after breaking the power of those who would make of religion an instrument of tyranny?

Let us look at the evidence of history. The Battle of Badr was the first armed clash between the Muslims and the idolaters. This was fifteen years after the first call to Islam had been made openly for all to hear! What of the condition of the believers during that period? In the Makkan society in which they lived their rights were forfeit, and they were the objects of scorn and enmity to all and sundry.

As the Prophet, upon him be peace, petitioned heaven for strength and patience, the idolaters refused outright to recognize Islam or regard it as a religion acceptable to Arabian society. The Muslims were banished from Makkah, the sacred sanctuary! Having thus bared their teeth, the idolaters announced that anyone entering the fold of Islam would find degradation and expulsion to be his lot. Under such circumstances can one possibly blame the Muslims for offering resistance to this kind of provocation? What could they do, save to await deliverance on some unknown tomorrow? And then one day, at a time when it was least expected, that deliverance came.

The Battle of Badr was thrust upon the Muslims by circumstances so unexpected that they had no time to plan or prepare for it. Indeed, a number of them were very much opposed to the undertaking. But, on came the idolaters, fully confident that they would rout the Muslims, and bury Islam deep in a grave of desert sand. The Prophet, upon him be peace, realized that there could be no escape from armed confrontation. The day had come on which all the bitter suffering of the past would come to a head, and the will of Allah would be done on the battlefield, prepared for that purpose by the divine decree. Therefore, the Prophet, upon him be peace, turned to his Lord in earnest supplication for assistance and protection.

Ibn 'Abbas related that, as he was in the tent erected for him prior to the Battle of Badr, the Prophet of Allah, upon him be peace, said:

'O Lord, I implore You to help us, by Your convenant and Your promise. O Lord, if it be Your will, You will not be worshipped after tomorrow.'

Abu Bakr, who was sitting nearby, took the Prophet's hand and said: 'Enough, O Prophet of Allah! Would you importune your Lord?

But the Prophet got up and left the tent, saying:

'The hosts shall be routed, and they shall turn their backs [in flight]'. (al Qamar 54: 45)

It is also related that the Prophet, upon him be peace, faced the qiblah, raised his hands, and began calling to his Lord, Exalted be His name, in the following manner:

O Lord, fulfill all that You have promised me! O Lord, bring to pass all that You have promised me! O Lord, if this group of believers is defeated, there will be no one on earth to worship You!

The Prophet, upon him be peace, knew that the Quraysh had advanced, in all their pride and vainglory, in order to crown their long persecution of Islam with one decisive blow. And, of course, he also knew that the fledgling Muslim community had patiently suffered all manner of hardship and deprivation while steadfastly adhering to the new religion in the face of severe opposition. Thus, seeing the condition of the believers prior to the battle, he prayed:

O Lord, verily they are starving, so give them their fill! O Lord, they are barefooted, so carry them! O Lord, they are naked, so clothe them!

Indeed, their faith had demanded much of them over the years. Not one of them knew that the Almighty had already destined that their situation should undergo a radical change, that He had enticed the Quraysh into undertaking a military engagement for which there was no strategic reason. And that He had confronted the Muslims with a reality from which there was to be no turning back! Why so?

It is Allah's will to prove the truth to be true in accordance with His words, and to wipe out the last remnant of those who denied the truth so that He might prove the truth to be true and the false to be false, however hateful this might be to those who were lost in sin. Lo! you were praying unto your Lord for aid, whereupon He thus responded to you. (al Anfal 8: 8-9)

The All Merciful answered His Prophet's call! And so descended the unexpected victory like a thunderbolt to break the back of disbelief itself! Yet the victory at Badr was to be the beginning of a new era of armed confrontation between Islam and the forces inimical to it.

After the victory, the Prophet, upon him be peace, and his Companions resumed where they had left off, performing deeds that would earn for them both the pleasure of the Almighty and a place in His eternal paradise. Men of such mighty spirituality certainly had no worldly ambitions. Rather, the lesson they had learned so well from the Prophet, upon him be peace, was that to meet one's death standing up for one's beliefs is the most auspicious way for a believer to end his life. The believers took this teaching to heart at times of ease as well as of difficulty. Thus, we see them petitioning the Lord for martyrdom even in times of peace. In a hadith it is related:

> Whoever prays, in all sincerity, to be killed in the way of Allah and then dies or is killed, will receive a martyr's reward.

In another hadith, it is related:

> Whoever sincerely prays to Allah for martyrdom will be granted that rank by Allah, even though he die in his bed!

Such willingness to sacrifice for the sake of Allah shaped an entire community which stood behind its Prophet in support of the truth. As such, its members never thought of their worldly standing. Indeed, for the most part, their link with the world was fragile owing to the suffering and poverty it brought upon them.

On the authority of Anas ibn Malik it is related that the Prophet of Allah, upon him be peace, went out to the trench (being dug around Madinah in preparation for the attack of the Makkan idolaters) on a cold winter's morning to discover that his Companions were still digging, in spite of their extreme fatigue and hunger, so he said:

O Lord! the only life is the life of the world to come. Forgive then the sins of my companions!

They were busy digging the trench and hauling away the dirt they dug up, all the while chanting:

We are the ones who pledge allegiance to Muhammad! In jihad for as long as we remain alive!

The Prophet, upon him be peace, insisted that combat be employed only for the sake of Allah; never for the sake of transitory gain. Moreover, he cautioned his followers against initiating hostilities and against provoking their enemies into action.

'Abd Allah ibn Abi 'Awf related that the Prophet, upon him be peace, once waited, when was to engage the enemy, until the sun had begun to incline, then stood among his followers and said:

O you people! Never wish to meet the enemy in combat. Rather, seek your well being from Allah. Yet, if meet them you must, then do so with patience. And know that Paradise is to be found in the shadow of the sword!

Then he said, upon him be peace:

«اَللّٰهُمَّ مُنْزِلَ الْكِتَابِ، وَمُجْرِيَ السَّحَابِ، وَهَازِمَ الْأَحْزَابِ، اهْزِمْهُمْ، وَانْصُرْنَا عَلَيْهِمْ».

O Lord! Revealer of the Book, Sender of the clouds, and Vanquisher of enemies! Vanquish them, and give us victory over them!

The defeat of the confederates at Madinah is an astonishing event. All the forces of disbelief on the Arabian peninsula had joined to surround the Muslims in their city state. The Muslims found themselves in a position so vulnerable as to bring them to the verge of extinction. There was not a glimmer of hope that their salvation could be brought about by any save the Almighty. It appeared that the Muslims had got themselves caught in a trap that would mean their ultimate destruction. Yet, the humble Prophet, upon him be peace, expected the succor of the Lord to descend at any moment. The moment came: the confederates were taken unawares by the sudden churning of the atmosphere by gale force winds that ripped away their tents, overturned and buried their provisions and sent them scattering into the desert in search of an escape from the terrible sand storm that enveloped them and tossed them far from the secure walls of Madinah! From within those walls went up a cry of faith:

$$\text{«الْحَمْدُ لِلَّهِ وَحْدَهُ، صَدَقَ وَعْدَهُ، وَنَصَرَ عَبْدَهُ،}$$
$$\text{وَأَعَزَّ جُنْدَهُ، وَهَزَمَ الْأَحْزَابَ وَحْدَهُ».}$$

All praise to Allah alone! He has kept His promise, come to the aid of His servant, given honor to His legions, and defeated the confederates single-handedly!

We have already seen something of the trust the Prophet had in his Lord. This is further reflected in the *du'a* he used to recite when he went into battle:

$$\text{«اَللَّهُمَّ أَنْتَ عَضُدِي، وَنَصِيرِي، بِكَ أَحُولُ، وَبِكَ}$$
$$\text{أَصُولُ، وَبِكَ أُقَاتِلُ».}$$

O Lord, You are my strength and my support. Through You do I dodge, attack and engage the enemy!

When the Prophet, upon him be peace, sensed danger from an enemy, he would pray:

180

«اللَّهُمَّ إِنَّا نَجْعَلُكَ فِي نُحُورِهِمْ، وَنَعُوذُ بِكَ مِنْ شُرُورِهِمْ».

O Lord! We set You at their throats, and we seek refuge in You from their evil.

The Prophet, upon him be peace, would not tolerate jesting, disorder or shouting during combat. War is a serious matter, and to go about it soberly is more befitting to a soldier of Islam whose only concern is to promote the worship of Allah on earth and invoke His aid. At such times the believer must have a full appreciation of the power of Allah, of His favor and sufficiency, and of the need His servants have of Him. It is a fact that one of the times in which prayers are sure to be answered is while fighting the enemy on the battlefield.

Behind the front lines, the rest of the Islamic community prays to the Lord for the success of the armies of Islam. Thus, in their five daily prayers they add a *du'a*, called *qunut* (prayer of submission), and especially at the end of their *fajr* (dawn) prayers. Out of these, the one I find most suitable is the one used by 'Umar ibn al Khattab, the *khalifah*, and the armies of Islam which overran the empires of the fire-worshipping Persians and the Christian Byzantines:

«اَللَّهُمَّ إِنَّا نَسْتَعِينُكَ، وَنَسْتَغْفِرُكَ، وَلاَ نَكْفُرُكَ، وَنُؤْمِنُ بِكَ، وَنَخْلَعُ مَنْ يَفْجُرُكَ».
«اَللَّهُمَّ إِيَّاكَ نَعْبُدُ، وَلَكَ نُصَلِّي وَنَسْجُدُ، وَإِلَيْكَ نَسْعَى وَنَحْفِدُ نَرْجُو رَحْمَتَكَ وَنَخْشَى عَذَابَكَ، إِنَّ عَذَابَكَ الْجِدَّ بِالْكُفَّارِ مُلْحِقٌ».
«اَللَّهُمَّ عَذِّبْ كَفَرَةَ أَهْلِ الْكِتَابِ الَّذِينَ يَصُدُّونَ عَنْ سَبِيلِكَ، وَيُكَذِّبُونَ رُسُلَكَ وَيُقَاتِلُونَ أَوْلِيَاءَكَ».
«اَللَّهُمَّ اغْفِرْ لِلْمُؤْمِنِينَ وَالْمُؤْمِنَاتِ وَالْمُسْلِمِينَ

وَالْمُسْلِمَاتِ . وَأَصْلِحْ ذَاتَ بَيْنِهِمْ، وَأَلِّفْ بَيْنَ
قُلُوبِهِمْ . وَاجْعَلْ فِي قُلُوبِهِمُ الإِيمَانَ وَالْحِكْمَةَ،
وَثَبِّتْهُمْ عَلَى مِلَّةِ رَسُوْلِكَ صَلَّ اللهُ عَلَيْهِ وَسَلَّمَ .
وَأَوْزِعْهُمْ أَنْ يُوْفُوْا بِعَهْدِكَ، الَّذِي عَاهَدتَّهُمْ عَلَيْهِ،
وَانْصُرْهُمْ عَلَى عَدُوِّكَ، وَعَدُوِّهِمْ، إِلَهَ الْحَقِّ،
وَاجْعَلْنَا مِنْهُمْ» .

O Lord, We seek Your help and Your forgiveness. We are not disbelievers, but believers in You, and we sever all ties with those who disobey You.

O Lord! Only You do we worship, and unto You alone do we pray and prostrate ourselves. For You do we strive and hasten to serve. We seek Your mercy and we fear Your punishment. Certainly Your punishment will attach to the disbelievers!

O Lord! Punish the disbelievers from among the People of the Book who seek to block Your way, give the lie to Your prophets, and fight against Your supporters. O Lord! Forgive the Muslims, men and women, improve relations between them, bring their hearts close together, fill them with faith and wisdom, make them steadfast members of the community of the Prophet, upon whom be peace and blessings, help them to be true to the covenant which they took with You, and give them victory over Your enemies and theirs, O God of Truth, and include us among them!

Concerning this prayer, Imam Nawawi said:

The Khalifah 'Umar's version of this du'a, 'Punish the disbelievers from among the People of the Book,' was valid in those days because the Muslims were engaged in armed struggle with the disbelieving Christians. Nowadays, however, it is better to say only the words, 'Punish the disbelievers,' as the meaning is thus more comprehensive, and less specific.

I, however, must disagree with the Imam in his choice of words for the *du'a*, of 'Umar, with whom may Allah be pleased. And this is because those who followed the path of *kufr* among the People of the Book, in both 'Umar's and our own times, are the seed bed of the troubles which confront Islam today, and of the disasters which have befallen us.

Indeed, it is owing to Christianity that the forces of communism were unleashed in both the Soviet Union, where the imperialism of the Tsars in the name of Christianity drove the masses to the atheism of Karl Marx, and in the Islamic world itself, where the Christian imperialists opened the doors to communism in the same way that they opened them to Zionism. The disbelievers from among the People of the Book were, and continue to be, the most hateful of all people towards Islam, its traditions and its values!

Let us return to the jihad of the Prophet, upon him be peace, so that we may gain a better understanding of it.

The Muslims underwent a severe trial when the confederates laid siege to Madinah. Indeed, as the noose tightened, it seemed as if their souls would be squeezed from their bodies like juice from fruit. Yet, in spite of all hardship, the Muslims held their defensive positions and repeatedly turned back the attempts of the disbelievers to force an entry into the city. The attackers decided to launch the decisive assault which would assure them victory, the essence of their strategy being to breach the Muslim lines and make a way for the charging forces to penetrate to the very heart of Madinah. And so the defenders came forward one after the other to fill that breach. From noon until shortly before the setting of the sun the battle raged back and forth so that the Muslims were unable, owing to the threat posed to Madinah, to recite their afternoon prayers. Indeed, until the danger passed there was nothing that the Prophet and his Companions could do but meet the enemy blow for blow.

At sunset, the disbelievers finally despaired of attaining their goal and ended the attack. As a result, the Muslims missed the proper time for reciting the afternoon prayer. This delay, more than anything else, so enraged the Prophet, upon him be peace, that he said:

> May Allah fill their hearts and homes with fire for having distracted us from our afternoon prayers.

Ibn Masud related that when the idolaters prevented the Prophet, upon him be peace, from performing the afternoon prayer, he said:

> They have distracted us from the afternoon prayer, *salat al 'asr*! May Allah fill their innards and their hearts with fire!

These remarks deserve further attention. Insofar as the Prophet was concerned, the passing of the prayer time was the true ordeal. The idolaters had prevented him from leading his Companions in submissive congregational prayer, and thus wasted for him, and them, the chance to address the Almighty, to seek His mercy, and to be humble before His majesty. For this exemplary human being, the height of felicity was to lose himself in prayer, to commit his whole being to the worship of the Lord of all the Worlds.

According to the scholars of Arabic rhetoric, prolixity, in its proper place, is a good thing. By way of example they cite the answer of Musa to his Lord as recorded in the Qur'an:

> And what is this in your right hand, O Musa?

The simple answer would have been to say, simply, 'my staff.' But instead Musa said:

> It is my staff; I lean on it; and with it I beat down leaves for my sheep; and many other uses have I for it. (Ta Ha 20: 18)

Thus he prolonged the answer to prolong his interview with Allah. The opportunity of a lifetime is not to be so briefly set aside.

In the estimation of the Last of the Prophets, upon him be peace, prayer was that opportunity of a lifetime, a heavenly ascension during which he conversed with his Lord. It was for this reason that prayer was for him 'food for the soul;' and it was for this reason that he became incensed with the idolaters when they kept him engaged in struggle during the time for prayer!

Indeed, the relationship of the Prophet with his Lord, be His name Ever Exalted, is well illustrated by an event which took place at the Battle of Uhud where the Muslims were threatened with the worst kind of defeat, where seventy from among their best were elevated to the status of martyrdom, and where the Prophet himself, upon him be peace, sustained a serious head injury.

Yet, despite the rejoicing of the idolaters and their gloating over the Muslims' misfortune, the Prophet, upon him be peace, called his Companions together in congregational prayer to praise Allah for what had occurred. Imam Ahmad related that, on the day of Uhud when the idolaters had withdrawn and begun their triumphant return to Makkah, the Prophet, upon him be peace, proclaimed:

Form lines for prayer! so that I may praise my Lord!

When the Muslims had arranged themselves in rows for prayer, the Prophet said:

«اَللَّهُمَّ لَكَ الْحَمْدُ كُلُّهُ، اَللَّهُمَّ لَا قَابِضَ لِمَا بَسَطْتَ، وَلَا بَاسِطَ لِمَا قَبَضْتَ! وَلَا هَادِيَ لِمَنْ أَضْلَلْتَ، وَلَا مُضِلَّ لِمَنْ هَدَيْتَ. .!! وَلَا مُعْطِيَ لِمَا مَنَعْتَ، وَلَا مَانِعَ لِمَا أَعْطَيْتَ، وَلَا مُقَرِّبَ لِمَا بَاعَدْتَ، وَلَا مُبَاعِدَ لِمَا قَرَّبْتَ».

185

«اللَّهُمَّ ابْسُطْ عَلَيْنَا مِنْ بَرَكَاتِكَ وَرَحْمَتِكَ،
وَفَضْلِكَ، وَرِزْقِكَ . . .».

'O Allah! Yours is all praise! O Allah! There is no one to withhold what You extend and no one to extend what You withhold! There is no one to guide whom You lead astray, and no
one to lead astray whom You guide! There is no one to give
what You forbid, and no one to forbid what You give. There
is no one to bring near what You hold far, and no one to hold
far what You bring near.

O Allah! Extend to us Your blessings and mercy, Your beneficence and bounty!

«اللَّهُمَّ إِنِّي أَسْأَلُكَ النَّعِيمَ الْمُقِيمَ الَّذِي لَا يَحُولُ وَلَا
يَزُولُ . . . . اللَّهُمَّ أَسْأَلُكَ النَّعِيمَ يَوْمَ الْعَيْلَةِ،
وَالْأَمْنَ يَوْمَ الْخَوْفِ».

O Allah! I ask You for the everlasting favor, the one that neither dissipates nor diminishes. O Allah! I ask You for Your
favor on the day of need, and for Your safeguarding on the
day of fear!'

«اللَّهُمَّ إِنِّي عَائِذٌ بِكَ مِنْ شَرِّ مَا أَعْطَيْتَنَا، وَمِنْ شَرِّ مَا مَنَعْتَنَا».

O Allah! I seek refuge in You from the evil of that which You
have given us, and from the evil of that which You have kept
from us.

«اللَّهُمَّ حَبِّبْ إِلَيْنَا الْإِيمَانَ، وَزَيِّنْهُ فِي قُلُوبِنَا، وَكَرِّهْ
إِلَيْنَا الْكُفْرَ، وَالْفُسُوقَ وَالْعِصْيَانَ، وَاجْعَلْنَا مِنَ الرَّاشِدِينَ».

O Allah! Make faith beloved unto us, and beautify it within our hearts; and make disbelief loathsome to us, and wrong-doing and disobedience, and make us to be among the rightly-guided.

«اَللَّهُمَّ تَوَفَّنَا مُسْلِمِينَ، وَأَحْيِنَا مُسْلِمِينَ وَأَلْحِقْنَا بِالصَّالِحِينَ غَيْرَ خَزَايَا وَلاَ مَفْتُونِينَ».

O Allah! Let us die Muslims, and be resurrected Muslims; and join us with the righteous, neither disappointed nor tormented.

«اللَّهُمَّ قَاتِلِ الْكَفَرَةَ الَّذِينَ يُكَذِّبُونَ رُسُلَكَ، وَيَصُدُّونَ عَنْ سَبِيلِكَ، وَاجْعَلْ عَلَيْهِمْ رِجْزَكَ وَعَذَابَكَ... اَللَّهُمَّ قَاتِلِ الْكَفَرَةَ الَّذِينَ أُوْتُوا الْكِتَابَ. إلَهَ الْحَقِّ».

O Allah! Cut down the disbelievers, those who give the lie to Your prophets and who impede the way to You; and visit upon them Your punishment and affliction. O Allah! Cut down the disbelievers from among the People of the Book . . . O God of Right!

From each word of these *du'as* faith literally pours forth. Defeat might destroy the resolution in the hearts of men only nominally committed to Allah. But for those who have lost themselves in Allah, and sold Him their lives and wealth, their faith shines with uniform splendor in good times as in bad. Such believers remain ever constant in their acceptance of Allah's will and their bowing to His wisdom. This is the secret of the words which the Prophet, upon him be peace, addressed to his Companions after their defeat:

Form lines for prayer, so that I may praise my Lord!

187

I recall what the poet, al Mutanabbi, said when his patron, Sayf al Dawlah, had done something to displease him.

If the deed which brought displeasure be only one, the deeds which brought pleasure are numbered in the thousands.

The situation here is, of course, of an entirely different order. To the Prophet, upon him be peace, whatever occurred was the will of Allah, and only He knew the wisdom behind it. Thus, the Prophet never described an event as involving adverse fortune. Rather he ever sought refuge in Allah from both the evil of that which He gave and the evil of that which He withheld. For a gift might have a disastrous ending; and while deprivation might be painful for the present, it might well lead to good in the future. The believer's refuge, his fortress at all times, is Allah, blessed be His name!

The Prophet closed his prayer with an invocation of divine wrath on the idolaters. The reason that he included the disbelievers from the People of the Book in that invocation was that the Jews of Madinah had been awaiting the time when disaster would befall the Muslims. (Those of the Jews who had not converted to Islam, but clung insistently to the deluded belief that only a Jew could be chosen by the Almighty for the prophetic mission.) Without a doubt, the blow to the Muslims at Uhud was severe. It did, however, serve the purpose of shaking the Islamic community so that the hypocrites were sifted out, for, after Uhud, they appeared in their true colors. And the believers learned how to face events with ardent faith, and united ranks! The Jews did indeed exult over the Muslims' defeat with malicious pleasure. Yet it was only a matter of years before they were overcome by a disaster far greater, and were forced to migrate from the heart of the Arabian peninsula.

The historians often speak of Muhammad the Warrior, often calling him a military genius. Yet they commit the greatest of mistakes when they attempt to divorce this aspect of the man from the more important aspects of his life. Muhammad took to the battlefield only when the shedding of blood was the only guarantee of life for the community of believers. The military operations carried out by Muhammad and his Companions were undertaken in the way of Allah and had nothing whatever to do with personal ambition, self glorification, the expansion of empire, or any of the other motives usually assigned by historians to the outbreak of warfare.

It is reliably related that 'A'ishah, may Allah be pleased with her, said:

> The Prophet of Allah never raised a hand against one of his servants, and certainly never against a woman. Indeed, he never raised a hand against anything except to fight in the way of Allah. Nor was he ever given a choice between two things but that he selected the easier of the two; except that it be a sinful thing. For, indeed, the Prophet was the furthest removed of all people from sin. And never once did he take revenge on someone for something that they had caused to befall him. However, on those who violated what Allah had made sacred he took revenge for Allah most High.

The Prophet, upon him be peace, said of himself:

> I have been sent to perfect good morality.

Among the many descriptions of the Prophet, upon him be peace, is the following:

> He was neither gruff, nor impolite; nor was he taken to raising his voice like a hawker in the market place. If he passed by, a flaming candle would no more than flicker owing to the serenity of his gait; and if he walked over reeds, not a sound would come from below his feet. He never used obscene language. Through him the Almighty opened eyes that were blind, ears that were deaf, and hearts that were sealed.

In this same hadith the words of Allah Himself are recorded:

I direct him to everything that is good, I have gifted him with every noble quality, I have made tranquillity his raiment, righteousness his emblem, heedfulness his conscience, wisdom his word, truthfulness and loyalty his nature, beneficence and forgiveness his character, truth his code of life (Shari'ah), justice his way, right guidance his leader, and Islam his creed.

Leaving aside these hadiths, let us look now at the basic teachings of Islam; the starting point of the Prophet, upon him be peace, in all of his campaigns, the Qur'an:

As for the [eternal] abode in the Hereafter, We grant it only to those who do not seek to exalt themselves on earth, nor yet to spread corruption: for the future belongs to the heedful. (al Qasas 28: 83)

Quite clearly those who seek exaltation in this world, and who work to spread evil throughout its length and breadth will be banished from the mercy of Allah.

The majority of conquerors and military men of genius have been of the kind that would scorn the notion of heeding the word of God, and scoff at belief in the Hereafter. The architects of imperialism, both past and present, have predictably been of the sort who have no relationship with Allah, and no knowledge whatever of His way.

But the Prophet of Islam knew of no way other than Allah's, and never took up arms except in His way. The teachings of Islam are emphatic in their insistence that those who strive exclusively for the attainment of worldly ends, and deny the possibility of there being anything beyond this world, will never enter the gates of heaven.

As for those who care for [no more than] the life of this world and its bounties, We shall repay them in full for all that they did in this life, and they shall not be deprived of their just due therein; yet it is they who, in the life to come,

190

shall have nothing but the fire for in vain shall be all that they wrought in this world, and worthless all that they ever did. (Hud 11: 15-16)

Perhaps more than anything else, these elevated teachings reveal the truth behind the battles fought by Muhammad and his Companions. They fought, first and last, for Allah. And the Last of Allah's Prophets, upon him be peace, undertook his military operations in defense of the truth, in order to foil the conspiracies hatched against it, to maintain freedom of choice in matters of religion, and to ensure that the words 'Allah is the Greatest,' continue to be uttered by the believers without fear of a capricious tyrant preventing them.

Those who fight in order to hear their own names shouted from the rooftops, or to amass the spoils of war, have nothing to do with Islam, and not the slightest connection with the way of Allah!

But the Prophet of war was the Prophet of peace, as he was the Prophet of prayer and charity, of righteousness and heedfulness; a whole personality in which all the best human qualities were rounded to perfection.

Having explained the position of Islam on the issue of warfare, we would not be overstepping our rights if we were to ask the forces inimical to Islam to provide an explanation for their past and present aggression toward Islam and Muslims in all parts of the world.

From the beginning of its history Islam has come into conflict with idolatry, Judaism and Christianity. And have any of these religions changed their positions with regard to Islam, even after the passing of fourteen hundred years? Do they not continue to threaten the right of Islam to exist?

In India, where the majority of the population are Hindu idol worshippers, we regularly read of 'communal disturbances,' that polite journalistic euphemism for the wholesale slaughter of hundreds or thousands of Muslims. According to Indian Muslims themselves,

191

the killing takes place only in villages where the Muslims represent no more than one fifth of the total population. In villages where the percentage of Muslims is higher, such events rarely occur owing to the certainty on the part of the Hindus that their own losses will be significant.

Nearly a million Muslims fell victim to Hindu savagery at the time of partition and the creation of Pakistan. The hatred of Muslims and violence toward them in villages throughout Hindustan continues unabated even to this very day. Throughout all their bloodletting did the idolaters ever feel a twinge of conscience? Will they ever?

In recent months we have read about the slaughter of some ten thousand Muslims in Chad. It seems that this kind of ominous news is becoming common for Africa; ever since the increased tempo of missionary activities there. Undoubtedly, the responsibility for these massacres lies with the modern crusaders of Christendom.

A short time ago, in an Islamic country which is very dear to me, I spoke of these matters and then suggested that the Muslims set aside a day every year to commemorate the blood and religion of these Muslim martyrs from the four corners of the earth. In our times it seems that the blood of Muslims is the cheapest blood in the world. If an identical number of dogs were killed each year, instead of Muslims, the Society for the Prevention of Cruelty to Animals would raise such an outcry that there would be no chance of such a slaughter ever occurring again.

Midway through the fourteenth Islamic century, world Judaism came to life and recalled suddenly that it had some sort of connection with a land called Palestine. Thus, Zionism was born, and a staged plan of attack was put into action. Eventually, the Palestinian Arabs were beaten into submission. Today, any Arab home in which arms are found is razed to the ground. How many of our Muslim brothers and sisters have perished in the struggle for Palestine since the outset of Zionist aggression? Thousands upon thousands! And now the Muslims are supposed to forgive and forget.

The hearts of those who fought against Islam from the beginning continue to be enveloped in unreasoning hatred for the person of Muhammad and the legacy he left. Is it not strange then, after all that, for those same people to accuse Islam of militancy? Yet it is their hearts, and their books of deeds that are blacker than the blackest night! Can these oppressors be allowed to continue making truth out of falsehood and falsehood out of truth? Can they be allowed to continue debasing the noble and ennobling the base.

Muslims have been ordered to depend on Allah, and resist all coercion, as they have been taught never to accept tyranny, and never to compromise the truth.

And so, do not lose heart and never beg for peace; for, seeing that Allah is with you, you are bound to rise high [in the end]. (Muhammad 47: 35)

Under certain circumstances suing for peace is tantamount to the squandering of human and material resources; and is unacceptable except to the most cowardly and depraved individuals.

This, then, is the secret to the scores, rather hundreds, of hadiths and Qur'anic verses which extol the virtues of jihad. And it will have become clear, from what has been realted above, that jihad means struggle in the way of Allah, not for the fulfillment of ambition, or the satisfaction of lust for wealth, or in pursuit of fame, or in order to establish racial superiority, or for the purpose of attaining any other such worldly end. Rather, jihad is for the defense of *tawhid* against *shirk*, for the defense of human rights against the forces of tyranny, and for the defense of justice against naked aggression!

In an attitude of reverence and awe, we look back toward the men that Muhammad made; Muhammad, the lover of his Lord, the beloved, the self-annihilated in love for the Almighty, peace be upon him and his followers unto eternity. Muhammad breathed from his own soul into theirs and lo, they became lions by day, monks by night, preferring Allah in all matters over themselves, and ever seeking His acceptance. They were righteous warriors, firm and unyielding towards all deniers of the truth, full of mercy towards one another. Whoever died in battle became a martyr in the way of Allah; and whoever lived continued as a watchful defender of the word of Allah!

There are examples among them of men who tore themselves from the embrace of newly-wed brides, to gladly meet, in the way of Allah, the embrace of death. And examples among them of men, and their numbers were great, who bade farewell to their kith and kin, in a society where allegiance to kith and kin was one of the main pillars of life, and went abroad in the world to propagate the faith.

When I look at Muslims today I am amazed at what I see. How many have sold their faith for a handful of worldly goods? Or have spoken words of *kufr* to obtain a position? Or have abandoned the truth to die a slow death because to stand up for it would annoy certain of their superiors? What have these mice to do with the men that Muhammad made? In present-day Muslim society the greatest of all aims and objectives seems to be that everyone should own his own home, that every family should have its own car, that each family member should possess this or that, and so on. But then what?

Nothing! To speak of Allah and His Prophet is a matter for ridicule, or worse.

As for Muhammad, upon him be peace, newly-arrived in the city of his supporters, the first matter toward which he directed his attention was the construction of a place of worship! And while he and his Companions themselves performed the task of constructing the mosque, the work-chant that they recited was:

> O Lord, there is no life but the afterlife! Lend support, then, to the Muslims of Madinah and the Makkan emigrants!

The Prophet, upon him be peace, there raised an army to uphold the Truth. He said:

A single morning in the way of Allah, or a single evening, is better than the world and all that is therein!

And he said:

A single morning in the way of Allah, or a single evening, is better than everything over which the sun rises.

And he said:

Three whose eyes shall never see the Fire: one whose eyes were watchful in the way of Allah; one whose eyes were filled with tears in awe of Allah; and one whose eyes were closed against what Allah had prohibited them to look upon.

And he said:

A day's watch in the way of Allah is better than the world and all that is therein.

And he said:

A day's watch is better than an eternity's fast.

And he said:

Whosoever arms and outfits a soldier in the way of Allah has himself done battle. And whosoever loses a member of his family in the way of Allah has himself done battle.

And he said:

The heart of a man in the way of Allah is never visited by fear except that Allah decrees that he never enter the Fire.

And he said:

Anyone who reaches the enemy with an arrow will be elevated one grade; and there are one hundred years between each grade.

And he said:

The station of a man who stands in the ranks in the way of Allah is more esteemed by Allah than sixty years of worship.

And he said:

The gates of paradise lie beneath the shadows of swords.

Abu Hurayrah related that the Prophet, upon him be peace, said:

Allah assumes responsibility for all those who go out in His way: For those who go out for jihad in My way, having faith in Me and in My Prophets, I shall be responsible for their entering Paradise, or for their safe return home with whatever reward they have earned, or with whatever booty.

By the One in whose hands lies the life of Muhammad! Never would I refrain from going to battle in the way of Allah, if that were not difficult for the Muslims! But often I am unable to arm and outfit them when they are unable to arm and outfit themselves, and it is difficult for them to remain behind!

By the One in whose hands lies the life of Muhammad! I would love to go to battle in the way of Allah and be killed, and again go to battle and be killed, and again go to battle and be killed!

These hadith are quite aside from the verses of the Qur'an on the subject, and from the practical example of the Prophet, upon him be peace, throughout nearly a quarter of a century in constant struggle for the victory of Islam, as if he was a revolving planet, never stopping and never straying. Indeed, that is what an entire generation of believers did toward the laying of the foundations of truth and cementing them firmly for all time.

Woe to today's world if ever the police fall asleep at night! But the nights of Muhammad and his Companions were spent in safe-guarding the progress of the truth. The same man whose feet would swell up painfully every night owing to his standing long in prayer would, by day, stand firmly on the field of battle.

I should like to emphasize here, again, that compulsion was never used as a means of conversion to the faith. Indeed, compulsion has been dearly refuted by all the Prophets of Allah, upon them be peace. History tells us, on the other hand, that the forces of irreli-giousness were the ones who continually made use of this particu-lar means in their pursuit of plunder. Here, too, then, it is essential that we give Muhammad, upon him be peace, his due.

The basic teaching of each and every one of Allah's Prophets is the unity of Allah. Not one of them taught anything different; not Adam, not Nuh, not Ibrahim, not Musa, and not 'Isa. Not one of them ever taught that Allah has a son who shares in His divinity, let alone a third god called the 'Holy Ghost!'

This trinity business is nothing short of preposterous, contrary to nature and common sense! Thus, Muhammad had every right to call out the truth of Allah's Oneness, and to confront every obstacle placed in the way of that call.

The heavens and the earth and all that lies in between join in to call with Muhammad as he calls to prayer! If anyone should think that to be foolish, supposing in his turn that there are actually ten gods, then he is entitled to think what he likes. But no one has the right to use his power or wealth to punish those who believe in the unity of Allah, or for the purpose of sealing their tongues; and on the day that his sword breaks as he attempts to commit highway robbery against the caravan of truth, let him go straight to hell!

Nowadays there are any number of such attempted robberies underway. Here an attempt to persuade Muslims to abandon their religion, there an attempt to deny the truth of the message entrusted to their keeping, and another to convince them of the need to desert the Prophet, upon him be peace!

Personally, I have no doubt that the responsibility for these crimes lies with the communists, the Zionists, and the modern crusaders of Christendom! Yet, by the will of Allah, all of their attempts will fail. For, indeed, those loyal to Allah and His Prophet will continue to uphold their covenant until the Day of Resurrection; believing in Allah, and refusing baseless mysteries and the powers of evil!

It was the will of Allah that in the *kalimah* (or creed of Islam) the believer's profession of faith in the Oneness of Allah is linked inextricably to his profession of faith in the Prophethood of Muhammad. Obviously, this is owing to Muhammad's being the most vocal of all people in proclaiming the Oneness of Allah, and refuting all hints of *shirk*.

From him, upon him be peace, we have learned how to know Allah with the knowledge of certainty, and to love Allah with the love of eternity; as we have learned to follow him as he recites:

> Say: 'Behold, my prayer and my devotions, my living and my dying are for Allah, Lord of the Universe. He has no partner. Even so have I been commanded, and I am the first of the Muslims.' (al An'am 6: 163-64)

What do others say? Undoubtedly, they speak of things about which they know nothing. But already the date of their appointment has been set for the Day of Reckoning:

> Verily, you are bound to die [O Muhammad], and, verily, they too, are bound to die; and then, behold, on the Day of Resurrection you all shall place your dispute before your Lord. (al Zumar 39: 30-31)